M000024492

Mindful Resilience

THIS BOOK IS DEDICATED to my parents. My father gave me the gifts of being able to analyze what was in front of me and problem-solve in even the most trying situations. His dedication to his work and his own integrity have served as a model for my life. My mother showed me how to serve the world with gladness, giving of herself, and being afraid of nothing. My desire is to enhance these gifts for the benefit of all. To both of you, I give my deepest appreciation.

Mindful Resilience:

NAVIGATING THE LABYRINTH OF CHANGE IN TIMES OF CHALLENGE

PAMELA COTTON, PH.D.

MINDFUL RESILIENCE PRESS,
A DIVISION OF
MINDFUL RESILIENCE CONSULTING, L.L.C.
JEFFERSONVILLE, IN

To contact the author, please visit mindfulresilience.com. "Mindful Resilience" is a trademark of Mindful Resilience Consulting, L.L.C.

Copyright © 2010 Mindful Resilience Consulting, L.L.C.

All rights reserved.
Printed in the United States of America.
First Edition

No part of this book may be used or reproduced in any manner whatsoever without written permission of the Publisher. For information about permission to reproduce selections from this book, write to Permissions, Mindful Resilience Press, P.O. Box 3307, Jeffersonville, IN 47131.

Original Artwork for Cover: Penny Sisto
Cover Design: Pam Forsee Hogue

ISBN-13: 978-0-9845982-0-5 (softcover)
ISBN-10: 0-9845982-0-0 (softcover)

—

Mindful Resilience Press
A division of Mindful Resilience Consulting, L.L.C.
P.O. Box 3307
Jeffersonville, IN 47131
www.mindfulresilience.com

COVER ARTWORK

The book cover is taken from a quilt by Penny Sisto, an internationally known quilt artist. Her designs come, fully formed, into her mind, and she dyes or over-dyes the fabric, pieces the work, and quilts it, all in her secluded cottage. I commissioned this piece with the request for images of water and a labyrinth, but, like many other aspects of this journey, it came with a surprise.

The owl flew toward me as I opened the e-file and saw the quilt for the first time. Rather dramatic and in-my-face I thought, similar to how life sometimes felt during my journey described in this book. A bird who journeys during the night, able to make its way despite the darkness, the owl seems like a perfect symbol for the possibility of wisdom through the dark times, something we all seek within ourselves when moving through times of challenge.

Then I remembered what had triggered its inclusion. The first time I read through this book, written in small pieces over the course of a year, I was struck by how much I shared and how powerful the experience of living through those times had been for me. I felt extraordinarily sad and profoundly touched as I revisited the emotions I felt near the time of my mother's death. Late that night I heard, for the first time in my new neighborhood, the gentle hooting of an owl. Walking outside onto the front porch, I located the sound in trees just far enough away not to awaken my husband.

She had come. My mother loved owls and felt she, in a sense, was an owl. Surely she was wise. She was true to her owl nature in the darkness after Hurricane Katrina, as she determinedly rebuilt and helped others in Gulfport rebuild their homes and lives. Now again, she let me know that all was ok, sending her love, as she always did, during my times of challenge.

I had shared this story with Penny, not expecting her to incorporate it into the quilt. Surprises and gifts can be amazing. My mother and I had talked about doing resilience workshops together. Though I had not planned to teach together in this way, perhaps this was to be. And so it is, my mother the owl – on the book cover as a symbol for the inside where she plays a prominent role, herself a model for resilience.

She and I invite you to enter our world as well as your own world of challenge and the possibilities for resilience. The time has come when we all must learn to walk with clarity, calm, and competence in the dark night of life's challenges. There is a little bit of owl in each of us.

ACKNOWLEDGEMENTS

An incredible group of people have been essential in the writing and publishing of this book. I am blessed to share my life with Dr. Kevin Brown, who is both my husband and a clinical psychologist. His encouragement and support were consistent, his editorial feedback invaluable, and his depth of knowledge and understanding of people and mindfulness tremendously helpful as I developed and refined the core concepts described in this book.

I am extremely grateful to Dr. Susan Mayfield, Dr. Paula W. Sunderman, and Dr. Lynne Simon, who all gave generously of their time and knowledge. Susan's detailed editing, feedback about my concepts, and insistence that these ideas were worth publishing have truly brought this book to life. Paula's feedback about the flow of the stories inspired the book's current structure and greatly increased its readability. Lynne provided guidance about the more spiritual aspects and encouraged me to include times I struggled with mindfulness.

The book grew from a text file on my computer to the object you hold in your hands through the creativity and assistance of others. A beautiful quilt by Penny Sisto hangs on the wall in my home and watched over me as I wrote. I asked Penny to make a cover for the book, and she responded with another quilt which graces the cover and holds the book in loveliness. Pam Forsee Hogue was the graphic designer whose technical expertise and wonderful artistic eye designed the cover and transformed the text, creating something both professional and lovely. Geoffrey Carr's expert photography brought the details of Penny's artwork to the cover. Bethany Parks photographed me in the context of nature where I could relax and allow my real self to be captured on film. I very much appreciate the expertise of each of these artists and the commitment they showed to the development of this book.

My long-time friend Sean Gresh sent me a book on writing self help books, spurring my ambition and ideas. Scot Duvall helped with copyright issues and taught me about the trademark world. Blayr Barnard and the Small Business Development Center guided me in learning about social networking and marketing, invaluable assistance as I make this book available to those who might find it helpful. Randy Smith from Destinations Booksellers in New Albany, IN taught me about book selling and how to include independent bookstores in the sales process.

I am also grateful for the support and encouragement of family and friends through this entire journey of life transition and then writing. I greatly appreciate the incredible support of my sisters, Pat Newman and Nannette Pawlowski, and that of my father's wife, Paula Sunderman. There are no words to express my deepest appreciation to my husband who supported me every step of the way. I won't list friends who have been there for me, as I would surely omit names. Your love and support touched me deeply.

I also thank the physicians, nursing staff, therapists, caregivers, cleaning staff, Hospice staff, support group members, and the ALS association who helped me navigate the medical corridors of the labyrinth during my mother's illness. Your support and advice were invaluable as I made decisions with and for my mother as we walked through the ALS disease. Your compassion is truly a gift to the world.

I first learned about the concept of resilience through the writings of the late Dr. Al Siebert. He graciously invited me into his home for conversation about his work and encouraged my own interest in the field. I am glad that I had the chance to meet him in person and am grateful for both his significant contribution to this area of psychology and his personal encouragement and support.

I was introduced to the practice of mindfulness through the writings of Dr. Jon Kabat-Zinn. His books and recordings made it possible for me to experience mindfulness and share it with clients. His body of work significantly influenced the writing of this book, and I hope to meet him someday. I greatly appreciate the tremendous contribution his work has made to medicine, psychology, and the world.

Table of Contents

Cover Artwork...i

Acknowledgements...iii

PART I

CONTEXT FOR THIS BOOK

Introduction: How this Book Came to Be 1

   1: Using this book for your life 5

PART II

BASIC CONCEPTS

   2: Resilience... 13

   3: Mindfulness 15

   4: Mindful Resilience 17

PART III

MINDFUL RESILIENCE AS A LIFE WORK

Preparing to walk the labyrinth...25

   5: Mindful Presence: the simple practice of being
where you are.. 27

   6: Mindful Commitment-to-Transformation:
choosing personal development as a life priority.................................39

Choosing to walk within a path 49

   7: Mindful Alignment: clarifying values and
committing to them 51

   8: Mindful Discernment: deciding according to your values.................. 61

Moving with Grace 71

   9: Mindful Embracing: being present with
a welcoming attitude 73

  10: Mindful Equanimity: maintaining inner calm..............................87

  11: Mindful Embodiment: experiencing flow 97

Heart-based Relating along the Path 107

  12: Mindful Compassion-to-Connection: choosing
compassion and connection 109

  13: Mindful Awareness-to-Balance: balancing life 119

Reaching Into the Depth and Center of the Labyrinth 127

  14: Mindful Refinement: becoming the greatest version
of yourself... 129

  15: Mindful Attunement: welcoming the inner wisdom........................ 135

Concluding Comments 143

Notes...147

Part 1

CONTEXT FOR THIS BOOK

Introduction:

How this Book Came to Be

Many years ago, while practicing as a clinical psychologist, I discovered Jon Kabat-Zinn's audiotaped meditations[1] and his book *Full Catastrophe Living*[2] describing his stress reduction work. Curious about its impact on my life, I practiced the meditations and found the tape program helpful in quieting my body and mind and becoming more present with life. I began recommending this work to many of my clients. Those who regularly used the tapes reported increased calm and decreased anxiety, and they were better able to work with their emotions. This improved ability to manage their emotional states then allowed them to more effectively use the therapeutic tools and the processes we were working on together.

Using the tapes as a structure, I practiced mindfulness regularly for a number of months, but my formal practice faded. Informally, however, it seemed I continued to practice. I always valued listening, and my intent was to be as present as possible with the person in front of me. Though I did not put these words on it, my time listening to clients, friends, and loved ones became my mindfulness practice, and I listened as they talked about their life experiences.

Over time, their stories portrayed the world as increasingly more demanding and more stressful. Some people seemed to have a greater capacity to accommodate and respond creatively and effectively to life's challenges. "Resilience" was the word that most closely fit this capacity, one that I began to view as a core competency for life. Because I had seen a significant impact of mindfulness on coping in times of challenge, I explored both resilience and mindfulness, which I believed would have a synergistic effect if taught in combination. For a brief period, I read about resilience and joined a mindfulness meditation group for their regular sittings. The pace of change in my own life began accelerating and cut this process short, bringing a new perspective to both areas of study.

My husband had been unhappy for years living in a congested metropolitan area with cold winters. In the spring of 2007, he and I agreed that he should accept an offer to work at the Louisville VA Medical Center. By that fall, he was there, and I remained in Chicago to sell the house, pack, terminate clients, and say goodbye to a life of over 30 years.

At the same time, my father's health worsened, and I made numerous trips to see him, helped make decisions about his care, and provided emotional support to his wife. I am grateful to have participated in his end-of-life transition in February of 2008. After our house finally sold that spring, I finished packing our belongings, moved my husband from a rental apartment, and coordinated my own relocation. I transitioned my private practice and left for our new home in southern Indiana ready for some rest. It had been a long year.

Less than a month later, my mother came to visit. Our original plan was for her to have a vacation, but a few weeks before she came, she was diagnosed with a minor stroke. She arrived ready to recuperate and return to work through her non-profit organization, where she tirelessly served those in need. Her symptoms and medical needs quickly increased, and within a few weeks our lives began to revolve around the hospital system, finally moving her to inpatient care after her legs totally collapsed. While she received rehabilitation for her "stroke," further tests were done, and she was eventually diagnosed with amyotrophic lateral sclerosis (ALS) and given one to three years to live.

ALS, commonly referred to as "Lou Gherig's Disease," is a condition of the nervous system that causes the nerve-muscle communication to gradually cease. The muscles become increasingly weaker, leading to total paralysis. For most people, the mind is unaffected, so a person afflicted with ALS is usually totally aware of what is happening. I was in charge of managing her medical care and frequently helped with the hands-on care as well. It was emotionally the hardest thing I have ever done, watching someone I greatly loved, and who was so incredibly vibrant, slowly become totally paralyzed.

As her situation worsened and we both experienced increasing helplessness, I focused less on "doing" and more on just being with her – helping her, listening to music together, talking (as much as she could), holding her, and just sitting, watching her sleep. I now realize that this work was mindfulness practice. I took walks, noting the nature around me and taking in the cool fall air, feeling my feelings, and noticing what arose in me and around me. Sometimes, I sat up at night when she would go to sleep and simply watched her. Not yet aware how all of this was moving me toward the next stage in my life, I spent all of my energy showing up for and dealing with what was in front of me.

Through this process, I was honing my own resiliency. I learned to cope with having no long-time friends around me, a home with unpacked boxes, minimal time with my husband, and the fading of one of the most important people in my life. My mother was also my friend and spiritual mentor. As we had always done, we both used this life challenge for personal growth, being present and seeking the meaning in the experience.

Despite medications, she declined rapidly. She gradually lost the use of her arms and hands, and both legs. Her ability to swallow faded. Her speech deteriorated, finally becoming a whisper. Within five months she died, unable to breathe because she could no longer move her diaphragm. I was not present when she took her last breath, but when I walked into her room shortly thereafter, her spirit was palpable and extraordinarily large, as it had been in life.

That confluence of events occurring over an 18-month period was both challenging and growth producing, sad and touching, with times of great physical distance from loved ones and times of tremendous intimacy in the moments of many losses. From it emerged lessons of resilience, a renewed interest in mindfulness practice and living, and a career direction that integrates my personal and professional history.

Writing about the experience also called me to presence, presence with my internal self. The process required listening to my internal voice just as I listened to the need in the moment during those 18 months. First I tried writing something more academic, but it sounded stale and at times confusing. This was clearly not practicing what I had learned. I stopped trying to push the process and decided to simply be present with whatever came forth in the moment. I chose to write from my experience and my heart as a way to integrate the experience for myself and create a language describing it. Others' suggestions moved the focus to a more universal application. I believe this sharing of experience and the language that emerged will be helpful to others.

The next step will be determined by you, the reader, and how you work with what you find in the pages of this book. As with life, we cannot know what is ahead of us. We can only make the choices that seem best as they arise, and discover the next step on the other side of the moment.

Chapter 1:

USING THIS BOOK FOR YOUR LIFE

AN INVITATION

Your life is a blessing, no matter how hard it is. It is tempting to mentally step out of life one way or another, and not experience the show, this wonderful, varied, sometimes complicated and downright painful, opportunity we call "life." Do you dare let it in, open your eyes wide like the curious child, and savor the flavors, so many and varied? This body is the form in which you may do that. If there is life after death, it is not here with the losses and disappointments, pain and destruction, deaths and disfigurements. Nor is it here with the sunrises and sunsets, flowers and birds, loving and love-making.

Do you dare to put your feet on this earth and truly engage with life and its multitude of emotions and experiences? This is the opportunity of a lifetime – in a lifetime – your unique lifetime to learn and grow and remember your true essence.

What we call "hard times" are opportunities that push us to learn new ways of being and invite us to soar toward the heights of our greatest potential. Is it easy? No, but how we are impacted by an event is influenced by our perspective. It was not easy watching my mother become paralyzed and totally helpless, but I would not have missed those last few months of her life. It was rewarding, touching, and profound. Words cannot begin to express the impact. This opportunity definitely challenged me to learn and to grow personally, and one of the results is this book. Perhaps sharing my story and creating a framework of language can help you follow and better understand your own process. I invite you to experience my journey with me and decide for yourself whether the process might serve you as well, helping you grow to become the greatest version of yourself possible.

This book is about changing the vessel of your life. My friend Terry introduced me to this idea as she talked about how her vessel had changed over the years, beginning as a small vase. As her awareness and understanding of herself increased, her vessel grew to be a large urn, shapely and lovely. Then she was shown her potential, and her vessel looked like molten glass, flowing and changing with the moment, luminescent in quality. What does your vessel look like? You might see this in your mind's eye if you take the time for quiet reflection.

This book is an invitation, an invitation to step into life, being fully alive in the moment. Only from full presence can action be integrated in a balanced way with others and with challenging times, and only from presence can you find the true shape of your vessel and the luminous light of your full potential. Balance and attunement come from silence, from going within to your center, your knowingness of who you are and your role on this earth. That is the seed of life that you can nurture so that it grows into the magnificent you – the greatest you can become. I don't mean great by society's standards, though that may happen as well, but great because it resonates with your spirit and makes your heart sing.

Greatness and challenging times go together – often. I hope this book is helpful to you in not just managing these times, but in embracing the fullness of the challenges and developing yourself to your full potential.

STRUCTURE OF THIS BOOK

This book is divided into three main parts. You are currently reading Part I which describes the life experiences motivating the writing of this book and the different ways you might use the material. Part II briefly explains two concepts, mindfulness and resilience, and their synthesis into a third concept, Mindful Resilience, a new term I am introducing in this book. The chapter on Mindful Resilience briefly explains how mindfulness and resilience are related to each other.

Part III identifies different aspects of Mindful Resilience as part of a life-long journey of personal development that can be facilitated by the way you approach life's challenges. I elaborate on each concept using examples from my experience over the 18 months of my transition and the loss of my parents. These events are taken out of sequence to illustrate the concepts. (The linear order of the events can be found in the introduction.) Because these concepts are aspects of a journey, the journey of Mindful Resilience, it is easiest to read the chapters in order.

The material presented can be read on two different levels. First, on a cognitive level, you can focus on understanding the concepts I have presented and how the examples fit within each concept. You may then choose to understand how the concepts might apply (or not) to your own journey. The questions at the end of the chapters are offered to assist this process.

Another way to read this work is to understand and emotionally relate to not just the concepts, but how they encourage you to move into the moment, personally experiencing your own process. Exercises at the end of the chapters are offered to help you explore this approach to the material.

Because moving into life challenges usually brings us face-to-face with emotions, this second way of using the book requires some mastery of emotions. If you become overwhelmed when you move toward or into emotion, or if this book starts to overwhelm you, then it is best to stop and seek outside help from a licensed mental health provider. Perhaps the idea of therapy is scary or intimidating. If you carefully choose your therapist, it can be rewarding and life-changing as you move through the sometimes challenging work that it is. This book is not meant to replace that work. Choose the process best suited for your growth.

Each concept in Mindful Resilience was discovered through events in my life, but they apply beyond my particular experience. At the end of each chapter in Part III is a brief section entitled "The Broader Perspective" which helps you apply that chapter's concept to your life. I suggest ways the concept relates to resilience, then offer a few questions to think about and exercises to help you begin your own work with this material.

I use the word "Spirit" periodically as I describe my experiences and also as part of the Mindful Attunement chapter. I chose this word as a broad term for Divine Presence to respect the varied words and beliefs of possible readers, though no name can encompass the magnificence of what this word represents to me. One of my words for Spirit is God. You are invited to use whatever word you use to describe Divinity. If this concept is not part of your world view, I believe you can benefit from this book by seeing "Spirit" as a deep human part of ourselves we can access when we are quiet inside and our intent is clear.

Part III can also be understood as a process parallel to walking a labyrinth. The Merriam-Webster Online Dictionary defines a labyrinth as "a place constructed of or full of intricate passage ways or blind allays" and equates the term with "maze."[1] As the concept of meditative walking paths has developed, a differentiation between these two terms has emerged. Jim Buchanan in his lovely book *Labyrinths for the Spirit* provides a different definition: "The labyrinth has one path leading you into the centre and then out again. The way is not concealed or disguised by walls; it just takes strength of mind to accept the journey and stay on the path."[2] He differentiates this from a maze with multiple paths and the possibility of being unable to find your way through. I am choosing to use Buchanan's definition, viewing a labyrinth as a path, usually circular, gradually winding its way toward the center.

Walking this kind of path can facilitate introspection. When walking a labyrinth, you center yourself before beginning, walk a chosen path (the labyrinth), move along the path with awareness, connecting with yourself and sometimes with others in the process, and then move into the center. As with the process of Mindful Resilience, a labyrinth can be walked repeatedly, with new learning each time. The labyrinth as metaphor for the journey of Mindful Resilience is explained as the book moves forward. The conclusion integrates the concepts and puts closure on this work.

The beauty of any journey comes largely from how lives touch and gifts are shared on the path. It is an honor to meet you along my path, and may this work help you reach your own goals of personal understanding and fulfillment.

Part 11

BASIC CONCEPTS

Chapter 2:
RESILIENCE

Resilience is defined by the Merriam-Webster Online Dictionary as "the ability to recover from or adjust easily to misfortune or change."[1] Recovering, sometimes phrased as "bouncing back," is a valid definition and a place to start. Yet, bouncing back to where things were is, in challenging times, not enough. We can move farther, walking into the process of change and into ourselves, attuning our lives to the things of true importance, and developing our understanding of life and of ourselves beyond what was and toward what it can be.

Resilience, in the way I'm using it, is that capacity in all of us to bend and flow with life, to allow the creative spirit and our skills to interact in ways that move us through times that otherwise might be called "difficult" or "impossible." Resilience includes the courage to be the best of who we are and the willingness to persist through the toughest chapters of our lives. It includes making the best decisions we know how to make and having the sensitivity to manage a roller coaster of emotions – both our own and those of others - along the way. Resilience can also include gratefulness for the intensity and intimacy, and awe from the inspiration found in an emotionally challenging process.

Resilience also presents an opportunity for great growth and development. On the other side of a challenge or trial, we may find that we have grown as a person, becoming larger than we were before, or being qualitatively different, more centered or clearer about life's priorities. Our capacity for patience may increase. We may recognize new skills we did not know we had. We may develop new relationships, and/or we may feel more connected with Spirit, whatever that word means to us. When we are faced with change, do we dare to actually change more than is demanded in the moment, open ourselves to the possibilities of change and welcome the opportunity to delve deeply into life, into emotions, and into relationship with ourselves, others, and the Spirit of life all around us?

Choosing this path of resiliency is walking into the tempering process. Steel is tempered by heat, rendering it stronger and more resilient. We can choose to walk into the tempering heat of change with the possibility of similar results as well as increased clarity, compassion, and inner wisdom.

This book describes a way of walking into the tempering fire. It gives you new things to think about, encourages you to go within and clarify who you are, honoring your goals and values as you face your own challenges. You are invited to foster your own capacity for presence, for moving into life instead of turning away, into "the full catastrophe" as Zorba in "Zorba the Greek" describes life.[2] Hard? Yes at least sometimes, or so it seems. Interesting? Always. Fun, sad, funny, disappointing, infuriating, heart-wrenching, frustrating, and awe-inspiring — and sometimes all of this at once? Yes, and more.

Resilience, as a way of moving forward, takes us on new adventures in the world and within ourselves. It moves us toward remembering the greater self that exists and developing aspects of ourselves that we never thought possible. Journeys of great difficulty can offer gifts on many levels, both for the one walking the path and for others. And, as always, wisdom is found in the walking.

Chapter 3:
MINDFULNESS

The basic concept in mindfulness meditation is non-judgmental attention. Jon Kabat-Zinn defines mindfulness as, "paying attention in a particular way: on purpose, in the present moment, and non-judgmentally."[1] This practice can be done with whatever is in front of us, whether that is washing the dishes, feeling the body, listening to another person, or noticing the breath. The breath is often used as a place to start learning simply because it is always available. It is this simple, yet broad, definition that I use for this book.

Mindfulness can be a formal practice and also a way of life. In formal practice, we take time out of our normal schedule to do the practice given. It is often suggested that phones be turned off, the door closed, and time chosen where we will not be interrupted. This type of practice was both my formal introduction to mindfulness, and is something I do now because I value that work. This is a way to develop the skills which then naturally become more a part of everyday life.

Life itself is also a practice ground for mindfulness, setting the intent to be present with whatever we are doing. This is the choice to move into life and into the moment, whatever that moment brings. This is where we can smell the enticing aromas and the revolting stench, hear the music and the clashing sounds, taste the sweet and the bitter, and see the beauty, the sadness, and sometimes the horrors of life. This moves us into life and life into us.

In this book, it is life which is the practice ground for mindfulness, both when alone and with others. We may choose to be in life more mindfully just by deciding to do so and reminding ourselves to return to the present moment when we notice our attention has shifted. Formal practice is valuable also, and I am currently trying to do both.

Decide your path(s), make your intent, and start practicing. Perfection is not the goal. The goal is in the process, and maintaining the ongoing commitment to the return – again and again.

Chapter 4:

MINDFUL RESILIENCE

My curiosity about the connection between resilience and mindfulness led me into writing. While writing about my experiences and my attempts to be resilient, I realized that I had made numerous decisions to be as present as possible with the process. I noticed that I had spent time simply observing what was happening at the moment and trying to taste every drop of life that was being offered. Mindfulness was clearly part of this journey. As I worked with the integration of these concepts I now call Mindful Resilience and attended to elements of this process, the language that emerged described more subtle aspects of the journey. Mindful Resilience became a process of managing change and challenge as well as a way of welcoming and engaging the opportunities for personal development.

I define Mindful Resilience as the process, through presence, of maintaining emotional equanimity, psychological flexibility, and the capacity to function in the face of challenge, while moving forward in mental, emotional, and spiritual development. This capacity is developed over time and is not something anyone fully achieves. We develop Mindful Resilience through practice, both during times of challenge as well as during the times the world gives us as "breathers." Combining these two elements, mindfulness and resilience, provides a language that meaningfully describes the process of using life's challenges to enhance growth.

Mindfulness and resilience are processes which reinforce each other. Mindfulness enhances resilience skills because it brings clarity and equanimity to the process. Likewise, in attempting to be resilient, we must bring more focus and attention to the task at hand to meet the challenge. This, in effect, encourages presence or a more mindful state.

The idea that mindfulness enhances resilience seems fundamental. It is difficult to cope with what is in front of us if our mind is elsewhere. We also need to be present to manage our emotional states instead of allowing emotions to manage us. We cannot think or make appropriate decisions if the emotions themselves are "running the show." We have them, as part of being human, but letting them be in charge is like having young children manage a household. The result is somewhere between chaos and bedlam. Times of challenge require the increased capacity to think, make decisions, and relate to others, and emotional regulation promotes that capacity.

Another way of saying this is that mindfulness precipitates a shift in perspective, one that gives a broader perspective where we are not identifying with what is happening in our lives. This stepped-back perspective then leads to increased flexibility, ability to productively work with emotions, and mental clarity because we are not identified with the process. The paradox is that this broader perspective actually comes with moving into the experience, becoming more present with what is.

This premise is supported by research. Daniel Siegel in *The Mindful Brain* notes that benefits from ongoing mindfulness practice include increased ability to regulate emotions, an improvement in thinking, reduced negative mindsets, improved reactions to stress, improved relationships with others, and an increased sense of well-being.[1] These benefits point to increased calmness, clarity of thinking, and increased quality of functioning which can generalize to other areas of life experience and be more available in times of challenge. Some of these results directly suggest increased ability to manage stress.

Dr. Al Siebert, in his award-winning book *The Resiliency Advantage*, has described capacities that contribute to resilience in the face of challenge. These capacities include: problem solving, self-managed learning, curiosity, flexibility, optimism, positive thinking, and positive views of self.[2] The first four of these capacities (curiosity, flexibility, problem solving and self-managed learning) either require some presence or would obviously be enhanced by increased awareness of the surroundings and the situation. The second two capacities (optimism and positive thinking) could be attained, or at least enhanced, from the reduced negative mindsets Siegel claims arise from mindfulness practice. All of the results of mindfulness listed by Siegel likely contribute to a positive view of self, the last of Siebert's capacities listed above. Dr. Siebert also notes in his book, "…highly resilient people can dance and flow with disruptive change because they have many attitudes and perspectives that let them be both involved and detached from the action."[3] This perspective is exactly what mindfulness facilitates, one that is both present and at the same time somewhat detached because of the "observing" aspect of mindfulness. Mindfulness allows us that perspective out of which the equanimity, flexibility, and function more readily emerge.

The second premise – being resilient encourages a mindful state – can be seen in the opportunities for mindfulness that resilience seems to foster. Times of challenge often narrow the focus to aspects of life that are truly the most important. Distractions seem fewer even though more decisions are required. Choices, often significant, offer opportunities to clarify values, and actions based on these values often have significant consequences within a short time frame. The compression of decision making and need for increase in alert and focused attention invite the engagement of the mind with the moment. In an effort to be resilient, we try to live in alignment with our values, and we often actively evaluate our decisions and choices. All of this invites our presence in the moment, and our level of presence is likely to affect our capacity for resilience.

In trying to understand my own experience, I have developed terms that describe aspects of Mindful Resilience. As with any process, the "stages" are never linear, and we move back and forth among them as we move through the work. The stages also flow into each other and overlap to some degree, though I have tried to define and describe each one. Have I complicated the process with my wording? Certainly the inherent beauty of mindfulness is its exquisite simplicity from which all else seems to flow. However, in order to understand the series of challenges I faced, I needed a language to integrate the different aspects of the process. This language also serves as a way to describe this interaction of both mindfulness and resilience to others. I believe this process continues to be relevant as a way of dealing with the increased complexities of life and the accelerating process of change now facing most of this country's and the world's people.

The world is becoming more challenging: I see around me more, and more complex, distractions – not just television but Internet fantasy worlds that engage people's hearts and minds, money and time. We don't just have phones but multiple social networking systems that sometimes require other "ware" to manage the extreme amount of communications necessary to maintain them. Distractions from music or radio stations in medical offices take people's minds off of their situation, interfering with reading or mindfully preparing for a procedure or a challenging visit. I am not saying that any of this is "wrong" or "bad," only that the world has much more noise – noise on many levels – that distracts us from being present, being in the moment with whatever is in front of us.

Presence is a choice, even in times of challenge, but we need to be aware of this choice to make time for it, to create space for it in lives that, often suddenly, become full of complexity, decisions, and roller-coaster emotions. The capacities that can benefit us during those times can be developed at any time in our lives, and will help us navigate the calms and storms of life.

Part III

MINDFUL RESILIENCE AS
A LIFE WORK

Preparing to Walk the Labyrinth

Walking a labyrinth is a process, as is living a life of Mindful Resilience. As we begin, it is important to center ourselves and become present. In both the walk and in life, this preparation allows us to be more aware of each step and more conscious of what we find as we move through the process. We are also committing to knowing ourselves more fully and developing ourselves personally.

Clear preparation for a journey also invites us to set intent which directs our work on a subtle level. Mindful Presence moves us into the opportunities of life, including the challenges, allowing us to make the most of those times. Mindful Commitment-to-Transformation clarifies the responsibility we take for growing ourselves, providing impetus for the personal growth possible during challenging times.

Chapter 5:
MINDFUL PRESENCE

Mindful Presence is a lifelong journey for all of us. I had practiced mindfulness each day for a period of my life and for many years consciously chose to be as present as I could with my clients. Despite this practice, large parts of my life felt hectic. Driving in the Chicago area was always an attempt to "get there" rather than be with, much less enjoy, the process. Being with loved ones or friends sometimes felt more like commas than a true quietude. "Getting things done" was a never-ending focus to juggle responsibilities. This was less true in the garden where nature lured me into her own rhythm which is always in the moment, but the sense of being present reduced significantly when I realized the time, washed the tools, and moved into the day.

During the process of moving and facing multiple changes, I began making more frequent commitments – actual conscious decisions – to being present with life as it came to me because I wanted to savor the meaning and beauty of so many connections I cherished. I was leaving long-term friendships, gardens and land I loved and had nurtured, and a business that had been both a calling and a great joy. Then I faced the deep loss of both parents. I wanted to taste the entire process and kept returning myself to the moment in front of me because I wanted to fully experience this suddenly time-limited life.

I savored the hours with friends, face-to-face time that I knew would be much reduced once I moved. Time with my husband was so lovely, as we were apart for many months and then, during my mother's illness, he so patiently waited as she became the clear priority. Sometimes he and I just sat together, or walked in silence, as presence does not require activity or even speech.

Others were slipping away on a permanent basis. Age had taken its toll on my parents, especially my father who fell and then required a series of back surgeries. Time with him served as another mindfulness training ground for me. My father walked with a walker and, due to a degenerating spine, was in constant pain even with medication. His mental capacity was fading, though it was impossible to tell how much of this limitation was dementia and how much was due to his incessant pain or his pain medication. Because of these limitations, helping him do simple tasks took enormous amounts of time and patience. A trip to the store to pick out one item was an afternoon adventure. My training took place out of his sight, but it occurred none the less. On the outside, I was patient with him, helping the best I could at a pace he could manage. Initially this was frustrating and difficult, with my body wanting to move much faster, and my mind often wandering to other things. I would bring my mind back and try again.

I recall one trip across town to a store selling handicapped equipment. He wanted to buy a hand rail, a specific kind of hand rail. His wife and I had arranged for her to have the afternoon "off" so she could do what she wished. He was still living at home. Dressing and personal preparation were important, so we took the necessary time for them. Walking slowly avoided unnecessary falls which, at this point, could be crippling. We arrived at the store, and he explained what he wanted and why it was the best kind, his engineering logic shining through brilliantly. The clerk was wonderful, entirely patient (unlike my roaming mind at that point), and we made the purchase. On the way home, I stopped for gas. He insisted on getting out, which of course meant unloading the walker from the back and making sure he did not fall. Inside the convenience mart, I paid for the gas. He was looking at the candy. I was processing the data (in my head: "He is diabetic, so he should not eat any candy. So what else does he have that he can still enjoy? Not much.") I smiled as I watched him buy that candy bar – a carefully selected Hershey chocolate bar with almonds – and eat it with great pleasure. I understood. This was life, the small pleasures, and he knew how to enjoy them with gusto. What a lesson. Could I do as well with my own life? We drove home, my mind quieter, and both of us happy with the afternoon.

I would drive down from Chicago to help his wife for a couple of days as often as I could. Gradually I moved into his pace when I was with him and began to accept the situation as it was. As I did this, time with him became increasingly precious, and we just began to sit together, being in the moment.

One afternoon I joined my father and other family members on the patio at his nursing home. The courtyard garden was lovely in the fading days of summer. The container plants seemed happy and well cared for, nature-in-a-box. It was only a taste of the trees my father loved so dearly, but a time we all appreciated as the four of us (my father, his wife, my sister, and I) sat listening as my father talked about his work with NASA and Dr. Von Braun, his years at MIT, and his conscious choice not to participate in the development of the atomic bomb in WWII. His brilliance sparkled in the window given to us, a mind usually clouded with illness and drugs. Those plants lifted his spirits, a contrast to the sterile, though attractive environment inside the nursing home. The music of life is subtle – and lovely – invoking connection in all who appreciate it. And, by this time, my body and mind had calmed enough to totally enjoy that time with him.

Later in the year, he and I sat on the swing at the edge of "his forest," the stand of maples, sycamores, oaks, and red buds in his backyard. It was autumn, and the trees were lovely in their going-into-winter colors, dressed in reds, golds, oranges, and browns. He could identify many of the trees from just their shapes or bark. Other than his wife, these were his soul-mates. And dedicated friends they were, always there for his soul every time he could walk among them or see them from a distance. He commented later that though he could not physically walk among the trees anymore, he would go there in his mind. As we sat, we reminisced about the hours we hiked together in my childhood, digging sassafras roots for tea and scouting for mistletoe and holly branches during the Christmas season. Time almost stopped as we sat unrushed, taking in the beauty. He had taught me about nature, and his later years had taught me much about patience and presence.

The snows came. Making a conscious decision to be as present as possible with everything, I began the last drive down to help with my father. Even the telephone poles, trees stripped naked and then creosote-coated, whispered a beauty as I watched their rhythm against the bleak winter stretches beside highway 65. It would be the last time to see him alive, and I knew that on a deep level. The stark winter forms of the living trees, arms reaching skyward, told their stories. Some were still fully formed. Others, coping with the prairie winds, were bent or – limbs lost or fallen – misshapen, as we can become. Leaves would sprout on many in the spring, alive and dancing in the breezes, despite hardships and the toll of time. I felt a connection with these trees, these friends of my father's, as though their resilience had much to teach my soul. "It is ok. We know the way," they whispered to my heavy heart. Tears, a faint smile, and great appreciation for their existence was my reply. As dusk rolled in, the sunset showed itself in its oranges and pinks as life and its colors faded around me.

When I walked into my father's hospital room, he struggled to see through his fog of pain and then let me know how grateful he was that I had come. His wispy white hair framed his contorted face as waves of pain seemed to push into his consciousness from his now advanced cancer. Without a new prescription, the nursing staff could not increase his medication, and the doctor was not returning the page, apparently due to a malfunctioning pager. Since touch seemed to increase his discomfort, we used loving words and Healing Touch to help him relax and help ourselves feel useful. He had been one of my first "guinea pigs" when I learned Healing Touch years before, fully open to my helping on this subtle level as he came out of a near-death surgery for a bleeding ulcer. Despite his left-brain engineering and science background, he supported my new hobby of experimenting with this ancient form of healing that had been initiated in the nursing profession.

When the doctor was able to respond, she placed an order, allowing the morphine to be given in gradually increasing dosages until the pain was managed. As my father's pain subsided, his body relaxed, and his face emanated peace. His wife and I sat with him throughout the rest of the day and evening. The recollection of these moments brings tears to my eyes and sadness in my body. Being present in the moment at that time and now as the sad feelings arise is, to me, part of the beauty of life. Being present isn't about feeling good, but about being fully in life's moment, treating it as the gift it is.

How do I put into words such a profound experience as witnessing the hours around a transition from life to death? For me, it was serene and sad, with deep connection in the touches of comfort we could give him in his last hours. And the silence afterward... Death has its own silence, deep and haunting. I still miss him.

His wife and I sat with him in that silence, grieving and comforting each other. Death was the midwife of increased intimacy between us as we shared tears and memories. My father and his wife also had great love for each other, and it was touching to have witnessed their depth of caring in those last days.

In the midst of my grief, I was trying to be fully present, but being present in challenging times is about intent, not perfection. As we drove home from the hospital a few hours before dawn, I stopped at a red light. A man standing on a sidewalk to my right seemed to be waving me to move on, but I waited until the light turned green. Within a block, flashing red lights appeared in my rear view mirror. Confused, I pulled over. The policeman appeared at my window and told me that my headlights were not on. This is what the man on the corner had been trying to show me. I apologized and began crying. When my father's wife informed him that we had just come from the death of my father, his voice tone changed. With compassion, he asked if I could drive home, and I agreed – slowly with my lights on – being as present as I could.

The gift of snow greeted me upon my return to Chicago. My driveway had been ploughed, but the hill of ploughed snow against the garage had hardened with the cold into a crusty wall by late evening when I arrived. Weary and cold, I shoveled the ice-stiffened snow so I could park the car under a protected roof. Having decided to just be present, I had no particular reaction. I just began shoveling. It just was what it was. The snow and I had been developing an even stronger relationship that winter. The snowfalls were frequent, and I was grateful for the gift of quiet that would come around me in the muffled sound and in me, as I watched the snowfall and then the blanket of crystalline beauty in our large backyard. Because the backyard was surrounded by a strip of wilderness (a natural area loved by wildlife), I felt isolated from the rest of the world and its demands. I could take long breaks from packing, cleaning, and closing a business to soak in the wonder of the snow's crystals. Each snowflake is different, like each moment, an opportunity for wonder.

PRACTICING MINDFUL PRESENCE

So, did I "practice" mindfulness? Not formally, watching my breath for 20 minutes daily. What I did was watch the snowfalls for extended periods when I took breaks from moving preparations and trips to visit my father and husband. I would be with my father, watching with patience (ultimately) and love as he very slowly picked out the apples he wanted from the store – only Fuji because that was his favorite. He would ask questions of the produce manager to make sure he was getting the freshest and best. That was his way of being in the moment and perhaps his version of mindfulness. We would enjoy together whatever nature was available, especially the trees which he could often identify year round. I would take walks with my husband, finding the bits of nature near our temporary apartment, appreciating how the sun filtered through the trees, or how the light was transitioning as it changed its position in the sky. Fingers entwined or walking side by side, sometimes we would talk and share, and sometimes just walk, taking in the morning or evening together. And later I spent long hours with my mother, helping her as needed, sitting with her, watching. All of this, I believe, was mindfulness practice. We always have the option of presence available, each moment an opportunity. The experience of being in the moment became a friend. It felt as though, in the difficulty, the present moment became more alive as I opened to the experience, because that is all there was - and all there is.

The Broader Perspective

Each of us chooses the degree to which we embrace the moment. Where is your mind most of the time? Are you in the past, focused on regret, fond memories, or old anger? Or are you in the future, focused on fear, dreams, or fantasies? Other ways of not being present are to put activities or substances between you and the moment in front of you. Perhaps you seek refuge from feelings by shopping, drinking alcohol, watching TV, or surfing the Internet. None of these activities is "bad," and certainly there are times you may want to reminisce, learn from the past, or plan for the future. Each of these actions can distract you from being in the moment. Which activities do you consciously choose? How often do you mindlessly do what is in front of you, or what advertising is enticing you to do, because you allow yourself to be pulled unconsciously into the next wonderful possession, interesting movie, or engaging activity?

Everyday life has vast potential for presence. It is easy to forget how profound it can be when you are scattered among activities, most of which appear trivial. But are they? Is it trivial when you shake someone's hand and look them in the eye? Is it trivial when you cook a nutritious meal for people you love? Is it trivial when you water a plant? And yet you lose focus – and choose activities that keep you from diving into the depths. Perhaps you avoid eye contact. Maybe you water the plants or cook in a mindless way. Perhaps you drive without really looking at the beauty around you. You slip back into mindlessness; we all do.

Because mindfulness can be practiced anywhere, at any time, by anyone, it is a tool available to us even in the hardest moments. Because trying times often push the capacity for effectively managing life, you have to focus in order just to cope with what is in front of you. I invite you to return to Mindful Presence, noticing and accepting the moments around you, just as they are. Who are you talking to? Are you making eye contact, and are you really listening? Can you accept and welcome the person in front of you even when you disagree with their perspective on a subject, or on many subjects? Are you exercising care in your actions toward others? And how do you use your time? How present are you? We must walk into the moment fully to receive life's gifts. Life awaits our embrace.

QUESTIONS YOU MIGHT CONSIDER:

✳ How much do you decide your life, and how much are you on automatic pilot?

✳ What would your life be like if you were totally present each moment?

✳ What is an area of your life where you would like to practice Mindful Presence, something you can do every day?

✳ What phrase could you use during the day to remind yourself to be more present?

MINDFUL PRESENCE EXERCISES:

Presence is about being in connection with and fully present with what is, no matter what it is. In the movie "The Last Samurai," Katsumoto spent his life looking for the perfect cherry blossom. As he was dying, he realized that every cherry blossom is perfect.[1] In this same way, each moment is perfect, perfect in what it offers. Mindfulness is non-judging, in essence accepting that each moment is perfect, and Mindful Presence is about being with what is without judging it, neither good nor bad. It just is what it is.

The exercises below and at the end of each chapter are intended to help you turn to the moment and become more present. Being present may lead you to feel more of your emotions. Looking at emotions mindfully, you may find that they are simply body states that move through you. The questions and exercises are offered as a gift and not as obligations. Choose what is right for you and how deeply you go into this material.

Mindful Presence is practiced every time you do any mindfulness practice, whether you choose to be present with your breath, your mind, a sensation in the body, or the life situation in front of you. Begin with presence. Practice with non-judgment. Just notice. The mind may continue to judge. What is important is to see it for what it is, as judgment or a thought, not identifying with it as part of you. These exercises are designed so you can return to them as you move deeper into your personal work, so this process may look different each time you try it.

JUST NOTICE: Open your eyes. What do you see in front of you? Just notice it. When your mind starts to wander (which it will), bring it back gently and with compassion, and return to noticing what you see in front of you. Look as though you have not looked before.

TWO-YEAR-OLD WALK: Pretend you are a young child, and take yourself on a walk - sloooowly. See things as though for the first time. It matters not where, as you are to look at things as though you have never seen them before, examining the details and "the little crawly things" that we adults usually mindlessly ignore. If you can physically do this, allow yourself to move into positions you have not experienced. What does it look like seeing up a tree trunk into the canopy from the ground level? What does the underneath of the chair look like? Stop and watch the ants or worms. Bask in the sunshine or play in the rain, anything that puts you totally in the presence of what you find. Allow yourself to follow your curiosity; allow your breath be taken away in awe of what is.

SOMETHING THAT MAKES YOU SMILE: Look at something that makes you smile: a sunset, a child playing in a sandbox, a sleeping baby, or a silly picture. Just notice the scene or picture, being with it fully. If thoughts or feelings pull your attention away, just notice them, recognizing that they are not the situation in front of you and return to noticing the scene in front of you.

Chapter 6:

MINDFUL
COMMITMENT-TO-TRANSFORMATION

We are making choices every moment of our lives, whether we are aware of them or not. If we bring real awareness to our choices, by being mindfully present with intention, we transform our lives. Mindful Commitment-to-Transformation is an initial decision and then ongoing re-commitment to take full responsibility for the life we are living. We make a decision to fully mine the blessings in the moments that feel delicious as well as those that feel utterly impossible. We are agreeing to be here with purpose, to become the best we can be and to discover that along the way.

Mindful Commitment-to-Transformation requires thought and presence. The more complex or important the decision, the more important that time be taken with the decision. Making decisions about changing our lives or ourselves in major ways involves "being," not just thinking. Just sitting, being present with the options in the moment and seeing what comes to us is an essential component. With significant decisions, we can do this in several sittings over weeks if we have that option. We can take the space that time allows, requesting decision time, if possible.

In the spring of 2007, my husband was offered a job in Louisville, KY. He wanted to move from the bitter and often snowy winters of Chicago to a warmer climate, and escape the hectic and sometimes intense traffic that almost constantly flooded the main thoroughfares of Chicago and its suburbs. After putting him off for two years because my psychology practice would be difficult to re-establish, I finally agreed to consider moving options. Stress from the cold and traffic congestion seemed to be diminishing his happiness in life. For over a year, he searched for other job possibilities, and now a real option was here.

We visited the Louisville area and talked with the staff at the VA where he had been offered a position. More importantly, we spent hours of quiet time together and alone both thinking and also just listening to our inner voices about what decision best fit on all levels. Neither of us had family in the Chicago area nor in Louisville, but Louisville placed us considerably nearer to several close relatives. We pondered the other most obvious factors, some pending changes with unclear consequences at his current job as well as a likely promotion there if he stayed. Another major factor was my leaving a clinical psychology practice and a professional network that supported my work in many ways, a practice and network that had taken decades to develop. We would be leaving friends, a home we had cherished and gardens that gave me great joy.

We also considered the intangible. We looked at our life as a whole. We wanted a lifestyle that allowed more time together and a less hectic pace. We simply sat – and walked – considering our priorities. In the end, we decided that a calmer life with more time for each other could be found either place because we would create it.

Then we considered the inner voices. What did they say? We spent much time just sitting in chairs overlooking the back yard surrounded by buckthorn and black walnut trees as well as Rogusa rose and other shrubs in the wildlife thicket that protected our plot of land from the surrounding properties. My large vegetable garden took up a major portion of the back yard, and the hours spent there had been full of joy and rejuvenation. We sat, talked, and listened to the wind. We both noticed – repeatedly – that, every time we moved toward deciding to stay, something in us felt we were to accept this opportunity to move. For us, Spirit was speaking. We sat with this experience, noting it, going back and forth. The call to a new life became so consistent and so clear that we chose to accept the offer and move. With that decision, I agreed to give up basically everything in my daily life except my marriage – and start over.

I have always been committed to growth. That decision first took the shape of formal education as a young adult. Then, as I moved into my 30's, the priority became personal growth. I strongly believe that we are here to grow and evolve on all levels, fully developing the talents we have. That spring, as we considered the move, I re-confirmed my commitment to myself. This move would be a way for me to grow myself personally, facing fears of change and reduced income, and professionally, by developing my interest in resiliency that I had been feeling was my next calling in life. Yes, I would leave things behind, but that is inevitable with commitment to growth. Yes, it would be sad and at times even painful, but it would be a time of transition to something – a more developed self – a more realized purpose.

I chose to commit to the growth I believed would come from moving into the unknown and being open to its possibilities. I saw loss in the context of the new shoots of growth that emerge from the compost heap. New gardens and new lives come when we set aside the old, turn over new soil, and focus on being present to the new situation. Then we envision where the new garden should be placed, what crops will grow best there, and when things should be planted for greatest productivity. I agreed to start over not knowing what would come.

That is the point. Walking into personal transformation always involves walking into the unknown. We may try to keep things the same so we don't have to deal with the uncomfortable – or terrifying – feeling of choosing the unknown. I remind you, as I remind myself, that change is a given in life. We never know what each day will bring. Can we live our lives open to this opportunity and view it as a gift, challenging at times, but a gift none the less? Embracing the unknown can create opportunities that allow us to become more of who we really are.

Mindfully committing to transformation allowed me to see times of challenge as opportunities to learn and grow further. This intent integrated purpose into the moments with the greatest confusion and distress, widened my perspective at times when fear was most likely to make it narrow, and opened my heart when grief was more likely to close it. As I write almost a year after my mother's death, life continues to open its doors. I choose to step through – into the unknown – with a grateful heart, a curious mind, and a commitment to the transformation I know is always waiting.

THE BROADER PERSPECTIVE

Mindfully committing yourself to transformation sets intent for how you move through life. It provides an initial sense of purpose to anything you choose to do, including how you cope with challenges that come your way. It also provides hope because it is a game you can't lose. No matter what happens to you or anyone else, you can grow from the experience if you have this intent.

There is also an opening to life that comes with this commitment. Curiosity naturally increases because you are looking for ways to grow from the opportunities. Life becomes an opportunity rather than frustrations you begrudgingly tolerate. Because of this chosen perspective, criticism of yourself and the situation is likely to decrease and be replaced by an interest in learning and creativity.

Mindful Commitment-to-Transformation means stopping and setting your intent as you face what can feel like a daunting task. It may seem as though you are standing at the edge of a cliff, looking up from the foot of a mountain, or moving into a desert. All are challenging tasks as well as awe inspiring moments. When you dare to just be with what is, the gorilla you are facing often becomes a monkey, and sometimes a mouse. It simply is what it is, and your power is in how you choose to face it. Sometimes you have more choice than at other times, but everyone faces times when the only choice is how you choose to walk the path.

You are standing at the beginning of the labyrinth, and your intent for the walk greatly impacts your journey along the way. You can choose to walk the labyrinth in front of you as a chore to complete, but that is likely to be dull if not boring. You can also choose to learn about yourself, looking for opportunities to challenge you in new ways, and being curious about how you might transform yourself as you move along the path. This may be painful, but it will certainly be interesting. And – you will have gained a new perspective along the way.

QUESTIONS YOU MIGHT CONSIDER

❋ What does personal transformation mean to you?

❋ What has been your typical way of approaching challenges in life? How has this worked for you?

❋ What would you like to change about yourself?

❋ How would this impact your view of challenges that come your way?

❋ Choosing to know yourself is a courageous decision. How can you give yourself credit for this willingness?

MINDFUL COMMITMENT-TO-TRANSFORMATION EXERCISES

COMMITMENT LETTER: Write a letter that you may choose to send or not, to someone explaining why you are committing yourself to changing your life. Choose someone (alive now or previously) whom you feel would appreciate what you have to say and would value its importance. Write the letter without consideration of spelling or grammar; just let it flow. You can write this even if you do not yet know the direction of change. Writing gives form to your intent. Writing is acting, and by acting, you take responsibility for your life, creating it in alignment with the highest of who you are.

LETTING GO LIST: When we choose to change, there will be aspects of ourselves and our lives as well as material possessions that we will give up to make room for change. List some things you are willing to let go of for the sake of transforming yourself. The list does not have to be complete, only started, and perhaps some of these things will stay. This is a beginning commitment to the process of release that is part of the change process. Revisit and add to the list as you move through your own transformation.

SHAKE HANDS WITH THE UNKNOWN: Neither you nor I can predict the future, but we continue to move into it. Consciously deciding to move into the unknown is part of Mindful Commitment-to-Transformation. This exercise is an introduction, an initial greeting of the unknown. Sit quietly with the recognition that you do not know what is coming into your life or what will be taken away, and note any feelings you have, labeling them. (Take a couple of moments for this experience, and you might note your feelings in a journal.) Now bring your mind to the present, the room around you, your breathing. What are you feeling now? How does that differ from a moment ago? (Again, take a few moments for this experience, writing your thoughts if you wish.) What happened to your hopes or fears about "the unknown" that seemed so real a moment ago? How did they shift when you focused on the present? What did you learn from this exercise, and how would you like to apply that learning to your life? (Note that planning at times is certainly necessary. The exercise is meant to have you examine your reaction to the idea of "the unknown," not to question the importance of planning or problem solving, both of which occur in the present.)

Choosing to Walk Within a Path

Every labyrinth has a path to walk leading gradually to its center. Walking on the path, not across the labyrinth, gives the process meaning and direction. The path is indirect, as is life, and it has some kind of marker. Perhaps stones are the guides, or it may be inlaid tile. This guideline facilitates presence as we walk because we do not have to clarify the path as we go. We can then be more mindful and explore the process more deeply.

Life also has markers, our values which we choose consciously or unconsciously. Mindful Alignment clarifies our values which guide our steps and our direction, giving them meaning. Mindful Discernment moves us forward in life according to those values. As with the labyrinth, we move indirectly toward the center and depth of our lives.

Chapter 7:
MINDFUL ALIGNMENT

Mindful Alignment is the process of continually and consciously clarifying our values and committing to them. A value is a way of living held in high regard by a person. It is the life to which we aspire. Mindfulness brings an active presence and engagement to the process of choice. Choosing one value over another seems to involve judging and be inconsistent with the definition of mindfulness. It is more a process of awareness of our best and aligning ourselves with that reality. Mindful Alignment guides the process by encouraging us to notice our thoughts about values and our life choices, while staying actively engaged in the clarification process. Then we observe whether that choice fits what we cherish in life and who we are at our best. We choose our lives in a fully engaged manner as we move forward in the process. We remain both clear about who we are and also open to creating that which we aspire to be in the moment.

The challenge of aligning myself in this process began before a choice existed. My husband began talking about his desire to move several years before he began to actually seek other employment. He did not like the long commute in the ever-increasing suburban traffic, nor the cold and sometimes frigid winters of the Chicago area. I resisted. It would take years to re-establish the kind of network of professional support and client referrals I had developed for my private practice. Would it be possible at all? I loved my work and enjoyed living with the beautiful snowfalls and nearby treasured friends. And, the upheaval of huge change never has appealed to me. Why bother when things are fine the way they are? Too much trouble I thought.

I have always considered myself a somewhat selfish person. I grew up in the privilege (yes, I consider it a privilege) of a middle-class family and was sent to college by parents who paid for it (another privilege). I did not mind living simply and cheaply for a while, but now I was enjoying a good income and financial security. Though I was not a lavish spender, I enjoyed my possessions and did not particularly want to give up the comfort of this situation. I also was not blessed with the children that I wished for, so had not taken on the world's-hardest-job of parenting and the sacrifices it entailed. Quite honestly, I was attached to this privileged situation. I resisted leaving all of this behind when my husband, cold most of the winter, asked me to consider moving.

Yet, empathy was getting the best of me. Over the years as a psychologist, I had developed the capacity for appreciating the struggles and pain of others, and empathy eats moth-holes in the shimmering fabric of selfishness. Though the selfishness was still present, its fabric began to look more like Swiss cheese, and I started to face my fears of leaving this comfortable situation. First, I had to face the fear of having less money. What is not enough? Well, I had lived on less before. Then I addressed the fear of leaving my friends. I knew I would miss them, some of them years in the making, more like sisters. Well, there was the Internet, and planes and cars did still exist. And southern Indiana did have people – and potential friends – what a concept! The biggest fear, however, was starting over professionally. I could not imagine beginning another clinical practice because it requires much networking, then building a reputation and clientele. I began to realize that my professional interests were changing. For several years, I had wanted to explore the area of resilience, possibly teaching, consulting, and coaching. Would people want to hear what I had to say? Would I be able to make it work? There was only one way to find out if it would work for me.

Actively considering my values and their priorities, I came to several conclusions. First, my husband's mounting discomfort, especially with the cold, was more important than my enjoyment of the area and my comfort with our current lifestyle. Besides, our enjoyment of life together was tainted by his physical discomfort for at least half the year.

Second, I decided that the financial security of my practice was not as important as mutual happiness. Moving from the relative security of our circumstances seemed irrational, yet I valued our relationship more than the comfortable professional and personal nest I had built.

The third conclusion was that change was simply that − change − not the end of the world. My home, neighborhood, business, friends, colleagues, and possibly my lifestyle would change, but I would still meet interesting people, have enjoyable and fascinating experiences, and continue my path of personal growth. I also suspected that personal growth was more likely in the openness created by choosing change and the unknown. And, we would walk through this change together, a blessing that would mean more and more to me as the two years progressed. I had not highly valued change in the past, but now I would choose it as a value in itself because it would allow us to create a life where he was more able to develop his fullest potential, and we could have more time together. After all, I married him because I enjoyed him − and still do.

Thus, I began the process of facing many small decisions, always referring back to what I valued. How often do I drive down to see my ailing father, and to visit my husband who had begun his new job before our house was sold? What do I keep, and what I do I give away? How do I fit in seeing my mother on her 82nd birthday? Having made the large decisions about values, these choices were easier. I did see my father frequently, and I did join my mother on her 82nd birthday. Some choices I deferred. Though much was given away, I kept too much "stuff." Sometimes the choices tilted in the direction of moving on rather than taking the time to decide. Move it and decide later was, at times, a kind of decision.

The major choices about values also streamlined the process of setting priorities when the need for major decisions occurred again shortly after moving into my new home. The previous year had been long and hard, and I had planned, after my mother's three-week "vacation" at my house, to relax, move in, and get organized – finally. (I had a long-standing habit of current "projects" piled different places and was determined to "lick this Dude" – a phrase borrowed from my mother – and have more order on a regular basis.) That reprieve did not occur because life required choosing among the possible demands on my time.

My mother began having medical problems, and the focus shifted to her care. How do I manage ongoing ordinary life while taking care of an extraordinary situation? Unpacking boxes, organizing, cleaning, pulling weeds, raking leaves, and repairing things would, to a large degree, have to wait. I planted a few tomato plants by the time Mom arrived, and we pulled a few weeds the first week of her stay, but afterwards the gardens were largely on their own. Some time was available for project completion because I was not constantly with her at the beginning. A very kind bee keeper and I removed the large nest of honey bees and their significant honey storage from the eaves by the front door. We discovered the bees as the movers were moving everything into the house. Fortunately, nobody was stung. I chose to take care of Mom first, my husband second, and then prioritize everything else.

The one thing I did for myself at the beginning of her foray into the medical system was to spend some time away from the hospital. She was in rehab and had her own work to do, so first I just visited daily, usually staying a few hours to watch her therapy and talk with her. When she returned to the hospital for more tests and later, as her condition worsened in the nursing home, I felt I needed to be more available to her and shifted in that direction. I constantly ranked (in my head) the list of "to-do's" and determined what was first. Bills were paid. Meals weren't fancy. And, I reminded myself, nobody ever died because all the boxes were not yet unpacked.

I found it a blessing to have established the process of referring to value as the basis of choosing when I faced larger decisions. Once I was clear, it was easier to stay focused because I knew the direction I was going. Yes, I had feelings of sadness or frustration, but I did not move into regret or re-thinking the decisions. It became easier to focus, and the values gave impetus and momentum to the choices. Smaller decisions were more easily made because they were in the context of the larger frame.

Making the large decisions around values also gave me a new perspective on the move. The move and the complexities became a challenge rather than a chore. I felt I was riding an underground river of depth and quiet while my mind was dealing with the necessary problem-solving required to make the every-day decisions along the way. I found that underground river refueled my mind and body as I faced repeated challenges, surprises, complicated interactions, new people, problems to solve, decisions, and roadblocks. All else flowed from the values I put in place, not easily of course, and sometimes the flow felt like rolling rapids. I seemed to be steering, but something expansive was moving through my life.

Beauty emerged in this context of values and choices. When I drove down to see my father, his eyes lit up. He would come alive talking about chemistry or physics, or his beloved trees. Even when he could not recall aspects of his knowledge or what he read, I enjoyed seeing these remnants of the brilliance he had nurtured during his prime. The visits with my husband were touching and deep, treasured moments in our many months of being apart and of having little time for each other due to my mother's needs. I appreciated his ability to understand the deeper meaning of my experiences. The months with my mother were a gift of exquisite beauty, with shared moments weaving together sadness and joy, pain and relief, talking and silence. I am grateful to have been able to share those beautiful moments with those I loved, for it is the greatest value of love that turns those moments into diamonds of great worth, stored in the heart as memories, and as life well lived.

THE BROADER PERSPECTIVE

Mindfully choosing your values involves staying present with life and observing how you interact, then consciously choosing the values that you most admire. It requires being present both with your life and your actions, as well as your internal states in response to your actions. Only then can you thoughtfully choose how you want to live your life.

For your values to become part of life requires that you commit to what you decide. That requires taking responsibility for the decisions you are making to move forward in this way, being present with emotions that arise.

Choosing and committing to values is a necessary and significant part of your life's purpose which then gives meaning in the moment when challenging times feel most difficult. It is what makes this journey worthwhile because it is something nobody can take from you. You can be in a hospital bed barely able to move, but nobody can take away living your values with whatever physical capacity you have in that moment. It grounds you in the Spirit of life.

Choosing values is like placing the stones in the labyrinth or honoring the ones that have been placed by others. These values and stones are guideposts to the wisdom center, and you won't make it there without them. Choose them carefully because they are like beacons of light along the way. They will keep you from getting lost in the exhaustion, confusion, intense emotion, and loneliness on the path of life's challenges.

QUESTIONS YOU MIGHT CONSIDER

❋ What are the most important values in your life?

❋ How do you want to be remembered when you die? What legacy do you want to leave?

❋ Why do you care about this?

❋ How strong is your commitment to your values?

MINDFUL ALIGNMENT EXERCISES:

KNOW YOUR STARTING LINE: Developing a value-based life is a life-long process. Begin by becoming aware of where you are now. For three days (or even one day), keep a log of how you spend your time. Make a list of time by the 1/2 hour and log your activities. At the end of the three days, look at how you spent most of your waking hours, especially focusing on non-work hours. What values are reflected in how you spent your time? Remember, this is your starting point and not a reason for self-criticism. Just the act of keeping a log can make you more aware as you move through the three days.

YOUR BIG THREE: What are the three greatest values you choose to guide your life? Why? This exercise looks quick and easy, but it is actually thought-provoking and deep. Take time with it, revisiting it as needed. Writing about this process in your journal may be helpful.

LIVING YOUR BIG THREE: If you lived these values fully, what would your life look like? Write this down knowing that it can change as needed. After you clarify the intent for your new life, what is the first thing you want to change about how you live so that your life is more in alignment with these values? Remember, everyone is a work in progress.

Chapter 8:
MINDFUL DISCERNMENT

Mindful Discernment is the process of making decisions with presence and awareness once a value is clear. As our life energy flows, discernment directs us forward, making our values come alive. It seemed that, as the tasks became harder emotionally, mindfulness was more essential. At the time of some of the most difficult decisions, I was having powerful emotions of grief and loss. In order to honor my commitment to my mother, making the decisions according to her wishes and in line with my values, I needed to be able to feel, think, and function. Mindful Discernment helped my decision-making be more effective by facilitating both presence and calm.

Early in February, my father's wife called me to be the round-the-clock caregiver with my father for a few days in his assisted living facility. I had clients scheduled for the day after she wanted me to arrive, and I was trying to be consistent with them because of the significant transition we were making in our work together. I had also decided to be as supportive as I could to both my father and his wife through his transition and dying process, and I intuited that a recent fall was bringing him much closer. I chose to reschedule my clients and go to be with my father. Before I arrived, he was admitted to a hospital, and my caregiver role was no longer necessary. By following my values, I was able to share my father's last day with him, to experience the grief-filled gladness so much a part of that intimate experience, and to share this profound experience with his wife.

Another choice arose as we tried to sell the house during the worst housing market in decades. The property was "unusual," making it even harder to market and sell. Neither selling it ourselves nor working with a real estate agent brought in offers, even with a reduced price. We finally received an offer - much lower still than the current asking price. In deciding whether to accept that offer, we again considered our values. One goal of moving was increased time together, and my continuing to live in Chicago, even with regular trips, was not achieving that end. The uncertainty was emotionally draining, and the regular 6-7 hour trips were increasingly tiring for me. We decided that our happiness was more important than the finances. The real estate market was also not predicted to rebound for at least another six months, possibly longer. Having considered all of these factors, we decided to let go of the property and of our financial expectations, a decision that has served us well.

The new owner is a nature lover and is taking care of that special piece of property in a way aligned with our own values, and with his youth and vigor, he is better equipped to do so. The home we purchased better accommodated my mother's limited mobility and reduced the travel time necessary to care for her medical needs. Had we not sold that house, I would have been managing the upkeep and selling of the house along with taking care of my mother. The market continued to plummet. Though we may have lost some money, we gained so much more from the perspective of our values.

What do you do when living your values becomes complicated? Early in my mother's visit, and before she fell, my mother insisted on having a bath. Not a shower, which was available and would have been easier to manage, and not even a bath sitting on a stool would do. She wanted to sit in the tub and soak, one of her favorite ways of relaxing. I wanted her to enjoy her visit (one value) and also cared about her safety (another value). I expressed my concern about her weak legs, but she assured me she could stand up. I reluctantly agreed. Getting her down was ok, though I was not encouraged by the "thud" I heard when she bottomed out. She was delighted and reveled in the warm water, soaking in pleasure and warmth. Her face lit up with that angelic smile she had, and her brown eyes sparkled. I could feel her deep ability to treasure the moment.

Getting up and out was another matter. After the first attempt, we stopped and pondered the situation. We didn't talk about whether we should have done this, for there is no going backwards when in the moment. We just considered our options. Eventually, we broke it down into segments, first moving her to a shower bench (barely), then resting, and then standing. I was relieved that she was now safely out, but I also felt a heaviness in the trunk of my body as I realized that she was even weaker than she had let me know. I suggested that we try a shower next time. Then she told me that at home, she had proceeded backwards from baths to showers, to sponge baths at the sink, fearing even stepping into the tub and standing for the shower. Oh!!! Now she tells me!

Did we make a mistake? Was I as mindful as I could have been? I had noticed that her legs were weak, and maybe I had not taken that fully into account. Had I known more, or been aware of how weak she was, I probably would have insisted that she shower. It turned out that this was her last bath, and bathing was one of the few ways she pampered herself. I am glad she had that bath and that pleasure, since life quickly became more difficult and much more painful. I also made a decision to be more aware of her condition.

Sometimes it seems gifts are given that far exceed the simple decisions we make as we attempt to live our values. Considerably later in my mother's care we had begun using a suction machine because of my mother's difficulty swallowing, especially during meals. She also had mucous, from which she sometimes needed relief. It had not been a major issue, just something else that required occasional attention. It was evening, and I said I wanted to go upstairs and check my e-mail (at the business office available to residents and family members), something I did on a regular basis while I was living with her in the nursing home. I postponed my leaving because I was attending to some things she needed before I left. I suddenly heard a horrifying gurgle, looked at the terror on her face, and grabbed the suction nozzle. It worked, and I was thankful that a nurse had spent time teaching me how to use the suction machine. Would she have died? My worst fear had been, after reading the literature on ALS, that she would choke to death, drowning in her own body fluids. That way of dying felt totally repulsive and unacceptable, and yet now it was a real possibility. I had to face that I could neither choose nor predict how she would die. This experience had really shaken us both to the core. I was relieved and grateful for the reprieve. The nurses, helpful as always, worked with us to manage this issue, and it never happened to that extent again. I stayed because I was following my value of taking care of her the best I could, putting her needs before checking my e-mail. Was that deep river moving my actions? I hope so, and perhaps an intuitive sense had aligned itself with that directional force. I do believe in Spirit, however, and I think it also possible that something greater than all of us kept me in that room to help her. We simply do our best and receive the blessings that touch our lives in the miracle-like moments, bringing tears to our eyes and joy to our hearts. I am glad I stayed and appreciative of the factors encouraging that decision.

Values necessarily informed the sometimes intimate and subtle choices we made about her health care. Many years before her illness, my mother asked that I have medical power of attorney for her. We had discussed what she wanted, and I knew she did not want to extend her life with extraordinary measures. In this particular circumstance, however, some of the choices weren't obvious. With ALS, a feeding tube can extend your "life," but is it life when everyone else can move a finger and speak when you cannot? There is computer equipment available making it possible to communicate using eye blinks, and the speech therapist arranged for her to try one of these machines. Although she wanted to live, she had to choose between death and life with total paralysis. I helped her consider her options, not an easy experience for either of us. She changed her mind several times on this issue, but finally decided it would be too painful to become a vegetable. Decisions about the respirator were similar. It had to be her decision – no matter what I thought or felt.

The hardest, however, were the decisions concerning medication. She wanted no medications that would alter her mind. When the hospice staff recommended medication, I made sure she was told the impact on her mind – often to the frustration of the hospice staff. They did not believe that someone could die fully conscious. I could not rule out this possibility and felt this was my mother's choice, not theirs and not mine. She did agree to sedating medication at times, tried it, and then refused. What I did was support her decisions and educate the hospice staff about another way to die. Their approach and medication protocols had worked wonderfully for my father, but my mother had a different perspective on life – and death. When, near the end of her life, a hospice staff recommended a sedating medication again, and my mother subtly nodded (all she could physically do at that point), this was a very difficult moment for me. I wanted to make sure she understood because she was near death, and I knew it. It was not the time for complicated discussion. She knew the consequences of taking that medication, as I had explained it several times. She had also tried it herself. I decided (intuitively) that she was making her decision to transition her way, and I chose not to intervene in the discussion. I knew that was the last time I would see her conscious and able to be present, and I vividly remember the long, loving look she gave me prior to taking that dosage of medication. I, too, knew the impact of the medication. My value had been – and was at that moment – to let her die her way. The disease took away her control of her body, and my job (and value) was to give her as much control as possible for every aspect of her life and death. Though her decision did not match her original plan, she chose how to die.

How do you put a pause in a book? The moment described above deserves some silence. Please take a moment for quiet reflection, and then proceed.

Mindful Discernment is a constant practice during times of challenge, and we can only do our best. Returning to the guiding values lit the path over and over. I also believe that something else may enter when we align our hearts with love, as though the world aligns with us, guiding our steps even when we are too tired to guide them ourselves. And in the process we are changed. We become more of who we decided to be. I am less selfish than before, softer on the edges like a seashell washed upon many shores, and more trusting of the tides of life. Perfect? Hardly, but more willing to be tossed and turned, and further refined, as my being is caressed and sometimes shaken, by the oceans of life.

THE BROADER PERSPECTIVE

With Mindful Discernment, you are actively choosing to walk within the labyrinth's stones, on the path rather than across it. You are choosing the path that can take you into the center of yourself and of life because it is infused with meaning. You are also choosing to bring your heart on the path you are walking.

Mindful Discernment requires staying present with the situation so you can make the best decisions possible in the moment. They are not always perfect. And you may not even know for sure they are the "right" ones. Being present in the moment gives you the best chance of choosing clearly, especially when you may be receiving conflicting input, sometimes from the same person.

Values and living them refuel you when times are tiring and straining your resources. They can feel like a life raft in the midst of turbulent waters. They add clarity to the situation and to your thinking because they bring focused intent into the moment. Because of the clarity they bring, they seem to provide momentum on the path.

QUESTIONS YOU MIGHT CONSIDER

❋ What is the most important value in a current life challenge, and how are you living this value?

❋ How does this value support your life purpose?

❋ What do you want to change about your value system, if anything?

❋ What is the first step in that change?

❋ How are you giving yourself credit for the values you are living?

MINDFUL DISCERNMENT EXERCISES

DECISION AWARENESS: Pick a relatively simple decision you made during the day. How did you make that decision? Did you gather information? Did you weigh the pros and cons? Did you use your intuition? What can you learn from this?

A DECISION'S QUIET SPACE: Sit quietly with the decision you made and just watch what comes into your mind about the decision. If judgements come, just notice them as thoughts that come and go. Also watch what comes into your body and emotions. Just watch and notice. What did you learn from this?

CHOICE IN THE CONTEXT OF VALUES: Take that same decision and consider it from the perspective of the three values you clarified in the prior chapter. To what extent is the choice in alignment with those values? Sit quietly and notice, without judgment, both your decision and your values. Notice what comes. How do you think this exercise might influence your life?

Moving with Grace

How we walk along the labyrinth path is a choice. Mindfulness encourages us to walk with curiosity, which fosters an attitude of openness. Mindful Embracing is an attempt to welcome what we find as we move forward on the labyrinth path as well as inside ourselves. This welcoming can help us learn from the experience. Mindfully Embracing life with challenges is similar, though the welcoming process itself can be a challenge.

Walking the labyrinth allows us opportunities to be mindful of our emotional states as well as any details of the walk itself. Mindful Equanimity is a process of developing inner calm through observing and embracing emotions which are a natural part of life. Learning to work with the emotions we find along the labyrinth path or in challenging times, and staying present to the process, can bring a sense of flow, or Mindful Embodiment. At its best, it is a dance with life from which meaningful coincidences may appear. The open-heartedness moves us deeper into ourselves and toward the labyrinth's center.

Chapter 9:
MINDFUL EMBRACING

Mindful Embracing is being present in the experience with a welcoming attitude. That does not mean we have to like it or agree with what we perceive is happening. We can treat it with a kind of appreciation. I studied Aikido for a year or two, and I was taught to move with the adversary's energy rather than against it. In order to step into the flow of life, we must move with the experience. Resistance and opposition is the alternative to going with it, and the process then becomes having a "fight."

Had I resisted these experiences, I don't believe I would have been able to be in the moment, see the miracles, or experience the growth in my heart and spirit that was both the process and product of resilience. I would have spent all of my energy in the battle, and then missed the experience. Life may feel hard at times, but it is certainly interesting.

I began the journey described in this book by fighting it, digging in my heels for several years, refusing to even consider, to any significant degree, the option of moving. I dismissed the notion as illogical, period. I did not want my husband to suffer, and I felt sad that he did. My problem-solving mind simply insisted there were ways to resolve the issues without moving. And, I could list them. My husband was patient and persistent, and I began to be more present. I became increasingly aware of the impact of the cold and the commuting on his body and energy. I saw that my ways of coping with the cold, though effective for me, did not work for him and kept him from enjoying the beauty around us every winter. Gradually, as I brought myself to be more present to the situation, I began to appreciate his level of frustration. And then I agreed to look for other options.

I entertained the possibility of moving, albeit reluctantly. "Reluctantly" meant that I didn't give him a hard time about actually looking for another job, so we were both surprised when I suggested he apply to the Louisville VA as we examined the list of government openings. Despite my increased support, we had to consider issues at another level when he actually received an offer. We knew there would be no turning back once he took the offer and resigned his current job. We had to take full responsibility for the decision, pros and cons, and move forward. We decided to move forward and embrace the opportunity.

Over the next year and a half, I gradually embraced leaving my business, saying goodbye to friends, and grieving for the loss of my father. Though his loss was deeply sad for me, it was not a surprise, as he had been mentally and physically deteriorating for several years. Partly because I expected the losses to be over, my mother's illness and decline were the most challenging parts of life over that 18-month period. I was already tired and stretched from the moves and the death of my father. Learning to welcome yet another loss was not what I had envisioned.

How do I welcome the diagnosis of ALS? There is no simple answer to that question, but the word "acceptance" seems to apply. At first, the doctor thought Mom had Myasthenia Gravis and ran tests to confirm this. My mother looked at me and said, "This is crazy. What is going on?" And then, "There must be some reason this is happening." I was speechless and just looked at her. In that moment, quietly inside myself, the letters "ALS" came up, along with the image and name of Steven Hawking. That night I went online and discovered the meaning of "ALS" and the connection to Steven Hawking. I knew then that she did not have Myasthenia Gravis, but ALS.

My sister had come to visit that day, to be with my mother so I could drive to Chicago for a long-scheduled oral surgery, and to see clients and visit friends. The six-hour drive back up north gave me time to be with myself, for my inner process to reflect on and integrate what was happening. The oral surgery was cancelled by the doctor after I arrived in Chicago, only an hour or two before it was scheduled to start, giving me more time to process the intuition about ALS and also to rest. That unscheduled time was a gift.

I remember trying to be with the gravity of the diagnosis. She would die, first slowly losing the capacity to use her muscles, and then becoming progressively more paralyzed. I went from my mother's words, "we can lick this dude" to shock as I realized this was a terminal illness. I sat with God, and He held me gently in my numbness, but I could not cry. Exhausted, and grateful to be alone in my friend's house, I slept.

When I returned from Chicago, I found that my mother had been transferred to a rehabilitation center on the presumption that she had suffered a stroke, but the medical providers had yet to determine a clear diagnosis. They were still waiting for test results. I shared my intuitive experienced with her, and she just looked at me. I didn't push her to respond, knowing that she needed time to process as well.

We both jumped into "doing," she at the rehabilitation center, me on the Internet looking for options beyond just slowing down the process of dying, which was all current medical practice could offer (and I was not sure that would be a blessing). I did find some research suggesting an alternative drug treatment, and I put the data and research together to share with the neurologists. Acceptance of what I already knew would take some time.

As I saw her weakening in rehab, reality challenged my hopes that my intuitive flash had been wrong. I recall busting into tears once when I was with her, giving voice to my fear that she was going to die, and hearing her insist that she would get well. She gave it all she had in physical therapy and occupational therapy, and the staff loved her persistence and effort. She was doing better in some ways, but I also saw progressive muscle weakness. For example, her muscles began to twitch, an indication of reduced nerve signals to those muscles.

I was grateful for connections with Spirit. The church I had attended only a couple of times had already put her in their prayers. I prayed, sometimes in tears, and sometimes I just sat in the Presence. More than anyone I knew, she walked with God. Many people talk about Jesus; she actually lived what he taught on a daily basis, helping people in need at any time of day. She gave things away, often things she needed. She was surrounded by Spirit, the light shining in her eyes and on her face. Spirit was definitely present with her and in this process. I learned to let go and let it be what it was.

Her neurologist, with kindness and compassion in his voice, told her the diagnosis – ALS – and the expected course and possible treatments. "One to three years" he said and medication might "slow the progress." He was also willing to try the research protocol I had found. She, of course, responded by saying she was going to get well. For me, I was glad the diagnosis was not a surprise.

Again I decided to be as fully present as I could as we wove our way through the labyrinth surrounding her illness, eventually moving from the hospital and rehabilitation center to the nursing home. She made decisions, and we made decisions, weighing the options. ALS affects the motor neurons which then stop giving signals to the muscles, so a person gradually becomes paralyzed. I had to do more and more for her, since she was able to do less and less for herself. For a while, the "doing" of life dominated our interactions. I would walk into the room, and she would greet me with "Hello Darling," and then "what I need you to do for me is …." Of course she needed me to do things, and I was grateful to be there for her. As we continued to move forward, I continued to "do" whatever I could to find information, look at the experimental protocols, help her with eating or whatever else she needed, and communicate with the nursing and medical staff as needed. I brought her the alternative ideas she wanted to try and even moved her arms for her in the Chi Gong exercises she wanted to do. On one level, she needed more help as she lost more of her capacity to move. On another level though, my focus started to shift.

Mindfulness was first a way to cope, to facilitate my best efforts so that I could see better what needed to be done. Intense focus was required in order just to take in the information and make the best decisions I could, helping her as she could do less and less for herself. Then mindfulness became a way of praying with the moment, grateful for each moment of sharing with my mother and with the world. Life in general, not just hers, became of great value. Small things mattered.

The important things got done, but some things slipped between the cracks. Gradually, I made some decisions to simplify life. I stopped calling about the experimental research projects because they all seemed to be out of state and required a series of visits to the research site. We both agreed this was not a viable option given her condition. I moved other things into the non-essential category. For a short while, I came to the nursing home every-other-day, giving myself some time to rest. As the ALS worsened, I began coming every day and eventually moved into the nursing home for the last month of her life. I was blessed to have that option.

Being present with "doing" became being present with "being," and just sitting in the quiet of her favorite music or the silence of transition from her vibrancy to her weakness, and from her weakness to her death. Despite helping during the day and also at night, there were increasingly moments of just being with her, enjoying music together, holding her, or watching her sleep. When my sisters came, they became part of the gentle focus on the present moment and the sacred space created by that focus widened and included them. "Being" briefly moved into "doing" as the aides would come in to attend her, moving her with a Hoyer Lift, a mechanical device for lifting her between her bed and chair so she could receive some semblance of comfort. Then back to being – and the breaths in the room. The staff, whom we had both greatly appreciated for months, came closer into the circle, sometimes spending extended periods to find solutions to her almost constant discomfort caused by muscle atrophy and having no padding to protect her increasingly sensitive body.

As I moved through this process, my mind and body quieted, just appreciating the moments and this time with someone very precious to me. I thought very little about the future, except what was necessary to manage her medical care. The whole world seemed to be in the now. I moved in and out of emotions, noticing them arising – often in complex pairs or groups – and then fading away. To me, they were welcome, whether they were hers or mine.

I tried to be with whatever was in front of me at the moment, whether that be a problem to solve, information to understand, emotions to embrace, or relationships to cherish. The most profound moments of mindfulness were just being with my mother, holding her, sitting beside her, or watching her sleep from the small couch that also served as my bed for many nights. Simply washing her face with warm water was one of the few pleasures she had near the end of her life when she could not move muscles and was often uncomfortable or in pain from the paralysis. I would watch her face soften, taking in the moment, being present in the shared love.

I was just being with her, loving her with all I had, and trusting in the process. I loved her in the moment, and the actions came out of that place. That was the flow we entered, she and I, moving with what was in front of us, appreciating what we had, and trusting that, on a deeper level, meaning was there, even if we did not see it at the moment. The more I accepted, the more present I became, and being present then led to more acceptance. It was like walking into the depth of the moment, bigger than that underground river I described earlier. It was like dropping into an underground ocean, with a kind of stillness and calm that held my aching heart, rocking it on the gentle waves of understanding. From that place came the embracing. Each small moment was precious, "perfect" in its rightness. This was her way of leaving, and I had the privilege of spending her last months by her side. What an honor. What a gift.

My mother's own mindfulness also contributed. When she arrived at the nursing home, she let everyone know she was planning to "conquer this dude" and go back to her beloved non-profit organization that she and her best friend had set up on the Mississippi Gulf Coast. Despite her own challenges, she supported and encouraged the life dreams of the PT and OT staff, which she knew about because she had made a point of asking. She asked about the aides' lives as long as she could talk, encouraging them, and regularly told them she loved them, even when she could only whisper. She would look them in the eye – being mindful in that momentary connection, and they knew she meant it – fully. She was one of the most alive people I have ever met, and she brought all of that life into this dying process, mixing mindfulness with the powerful capacity to love she knew so well.

At times we laughed heartily. She loved the top-of-the-line massaging footbath she had been given by her friend Sandra. She described the discomfort that came with paralysis, and massage of any type brought a smile to her face. Though it was probably against the rules, we used it whenever she asked because it was one of her few remaining pleasures. I felt a little nervous when we used it because I didn't want this experience taken away from her. A broad grin would light up her face as I turned on the jets, infecting me with her happiness. On one occasion, I was carrying the heavy tub full of water back to the bathroom, and I spilled some water on the end of the bed which housed the controls for the bed movement. The bed started moving as if it were alive, jerking itself into contortions so that it was tilted like a fully elevated dump truck placing its load squarely in my lap. Fortunately, she was in the wheelchair, and we howled as it continued its performance, with me madly pushing the buttons to no avail. Finally, I unplugged the bed, and it immediately stopped, but nothing I did returned it to normal. It was well worth the hearty laugh even though maintenance men were required to restore the bed's original position.

We became helpless together. She could move less and less of her body, and I could not keep her from dying. As her diaphragm became paralyzed and her whispers more faint, it was harder for me to understand her and respond to her requests or communicate them to others. Even making her comfortable was difficult near the end. All that was left was presence, just being with what was. The depth and intensity of that experience is so hard to put into words. Feelings came: helplessness, sadness, joy of spending this time with her, awe that her brightness continued. These feelings were profound as I watched her slip away into full paralysis while her mind watched each step of the descent, unimpaired. All I could do was sit with the emotions, feel them as well as love her, and help when I could. While she could still talk, she at times shared her own feelings. We would just sit together in those moments. Occasionally she would let tears come, but that was not her way.

The time being present with her, and especially the month I lived with her in the nursing home at the end, was an experience I would never have missed. The intimacy with my mother was intense and deep. There was also something larger than the two of us in that room. I call it Spirit. Our ability to feel it was nurtured by the love we had for each other and the staff, by our willingness to embrace the moment, and by the quiet. The love and quiet created the space. The presence and embracing of the moment seemed to bring it into awareness. I am forever grateful for that time even though the journey with my mother through her ALS and dying is probably one of the most emotionally difficult things I have ever experienced.

And her death? When I first wrote this section, I left that out, as it continues to bring tears. Yes, I pull away at times. My mother gradually lost the ability to talk, not just because her mouth muscles would not function, but because her diaphragm gradually lost the ability to move, affecting her ability to breathe. Her breath became more and more shallow, and she died like a candle flickering and then fading slowly into the silent night. How fitting for a woman who brought so much light to the world, certainly a bright candle in the dark days after Katrina in Gulfport, where she helped those in need.

My grief was a mixture of the most profound sadness I have ever experienced along with total exhaustion, tempered with relief that her journey into helplessness had been relatively brief. My sister and I sat in the room with the body and with her spirit that I strongly felt in the room. We cried, shared some thoughts and feelings, but mostly just sat quietly, being with it all. Through my sobbing, I allowed myself the privilege of helping the aides lovingly bathe her body. Her "envelope" (as she had fondly called her body) was beginning to have blue patches on her back as the blood pooled. "She" was cold to the touch, and her face no longer looked like my mother. In fact, it was amazing how different and empty it looked. The shape was even different, more drawn, as though the life force itself had provided structure as well as life and light. This final act of loving care helped me make the transition to life without my mother. I sob as I write this, almost a year later, and I have no idea whether my words convey those profound feelings. If you have been through similar experiences, you will know that words cannot convey what silence can embrace. And so, I still sit in silence, just thinking about her.

Finding presence in the midst of challenge was a great gift. This gave connection amidst helplessness, internal stillness amidst great grief, and meaning amidst exhaustion and difficult decisions. Once I decided to take this journey (the part where I had some choice), I walked with determination into the experience as much as possible, living it as fully as I could. As difficult as it seemed at times, it was a gift and was filled with grace.

THE BROADER PERSPECTIVE

You are now walking the labyrinth's path, committed to the growth you find along the way. Mindful Embracing is a reaching out to whatever you encounter, perhaps only shaking its hand in introduction. Bringing a sense of curiosity to the encounter will allow you to engage the process, both what is happening in front of you and what is happening inside of you. How are you experiencing the sounds or images in front of you or the thoughts or emotions inside of you?

Engaging and embracing requires you to be present, both with the situation and with your inner struggles, and only in the present can you see how these two aspects of life are intertwined. So much of what you see is based on your own perspective of the world and of yourself. Do you dare to look further and then emotionally experience what comes up? Is this easy? No. But this is where you find the learning to which you dedicated yourself in Mindful Commitment-to-Transformation.

Welcoming the world can be its own challenge. For many of you right now, the world seems unpredictable, confusing, painful, and sometimes chaotic. Why would you want to welcome what feels like a tangle of troubles? Your choice is to welcome it and come to know it, or spend your energy fighting it.

Yes, minimize problems by solving them. Streamline and simplify your life if you wish to reduce the clutter, and some issues may fall away with the debris. This, too, is working with and befriending the issues. Facing life in creative ways requires presence with the issues at hand just to know what you are dealing with. If you welcome them as well, perhaps, in examining the challenges, you may learn more about yourself, more about others, and smell the roses among the thorns.

QUESTIONS YOU MIGHT CONSIDER

❋ What is in front of you in life right now?

❋ What happens if you let yourself welcome it?

❋ Is it possible to welcome tragedy?

❋ Have you ever known someone who could welcome challenges, or even tragedy? How did they do it?

❋ What are the thorns in your life right now, and what might the roses be?

MINDFUL EMBRACING EXERCISES

EMBRACING A SITUATION: Choose a current or recent experience that is slightly challenging for you. Just notice it as it is, present in your life. Examine it, noticing the components. Use descriptive terminology that is not judgmental. For example, you might say "time-consuming" instead of "difficult," or "requiring interaction with a person who expects you to consistently be on time" instead of "awful." Choose words that simply describe what is.

EMBRACING THE BODY: Now notice how you feel in your body. Whatever you feel is simply a body state. Again, use descriptive terminology such as "gray" instead of "gloomy," or "heavy" - like a heavy box - instead of "depressing." Notice it and notice any changes that may occur as you notice it. If you have a pull to move away, just notice what you do. No judgment. What you do is what you do. Just notice.

EMBRACING ANOTHER: Think of someone whom you don't like. Don't pick the hardest person at first, just a moderately difficult person. Bring them to mind and just notice. They simply are a fellow human being. When thoughts arise, apply the method of the first exercise above – just describe, noticing any judgmental thoughts that arise as just thoughts. You don't have to agree with a person to embrace them mindfully, accepting them as part of the circle of life. Only then can you successfully deal with them, whether that means working with them on a project or setting a limit.

Chapter 10:
MINDFUL EQUANIMITY

Mindful Equanimity is the ability to stay calm or balanced internally while being present with what is around and inside of us. It seems to be what Ruth Baer, in her work on a mindfulness scale, has called "nonreactivity to inner experience."[1] We might look calm on the outside by finding ways to distance from our feelings and thoughts that upset us. Perhaps we try to control our life and surroundings, including the actions of others. Perhaps we engage in fantasy, such as computer games or novels, or use food or shopping to maintain the external state of calm. In contrast, with Mindful Equanimity, there is a kind of calmness or "evenness of mind,"[2] both inside and outside, while being present with an upsetting situation or even upsetting emotions. In other words, the mind is calm and balanced even when we are feeling emotions internally because the mind is noticing the emotions and the world as we are feeling the internal states.

Emotions are natural reactions, and we will feel them. What we can choose is how we relate to them and especially how we relate to the body states in which they are expressed. During the times I described, many feelings arose, sometimes very strong ones. I felt sad many times, saying goodbye to my friends, my parents, my beloved gardens, and temporarily my husband as we lived apart for a number of months. Sometimes I would simply let myself be sad, especially after my mother died. I consciously decided to allow myself to cry as much and as often as I needed to when I drove to Mississippi for her celebration of life. (She, of course, never wanted a funeral. For her, death was only a transition and her body "an envelope.") I not only cried at her funeral – to the consternation of her best friend/minister who was trying to lead the beautiful service, but also one evening when one of my sisters and

I enjoyed a delicious Cajun dinner. I talked while tears streamed down my face the entire meal. My gracious and loving sister just listened, and I am grateful for her gift of compassion and caring. I also listened and let myself simply be with the emotions. I didn't expect anyone to "fix" anything, as there was nothing that could be fixed. Feelings simply are – just part of the moment – to be heard and embraced, and sometimes shared.

Embracing both hope and profound grief at the same time was emotionally challenging. My mother was determined to "lick this dude," and she talked in these terms even a few weeks before she died, despite all signs pointing in the opposite direction. Earlier in her PT work, she did surprise everyone by walking the amount required by the physical therapist one day, and she saw this as evidence of improvement, but she could not sustain it. My mother was one of the most determined people you would ever meet. She had set this goal for herself and, of course, attained it. Her body, however, was dying, and I could daily see the signs of increasing paralysis, decreasing ability to swallow, and her ever-decreasing breath capacity. Allowing her the right for hope while at the same time seeing the painful progression toward paralysis at times felt heart wrenching. I would leave her (when I was still going home while she continued her therapy) with her uplifting music, happy and hopeful. My eyes often filled with tears as I danced out the door of her nursing home room, filled with grief while still joining with her spirited quest for the turn-around. She forever wanted to help others, and she wasn't finished. She would probably never feel finished with life and the persistent dedication to serve and help others in any way she could. I learned to sit with these two feelings, and feeling them at the same time became familiar, though never comfortable.

Watching her become totally helpless was also challenging for me. My mother decided to go to Peru and visit Machu Picchu when she was 79 years old. Actually, she insisted on it, so I agreed to accompany her. She did most of the walks on the tour, omitting only the extended hikes. She was lively and engaging on that trip, and showed the energy and enthusiasm of several people combined. Our fellow travelers regularly told me they were amazed. Only a few months later, she met the devastation of Hurricane Katrina with the same energy and tenacity. She was determined to rebuild her own home and to help as many others as possible, and she did both. She and her business partner continued to run their non-profit organization, The Nourishing Place, designed and developed to assist the neediest people, especially the children. She helped unload trucks, took items to others, and guided help to the greatest areas of need and money to those who could most benefit. This dynamic woman who stopped at nothing, who was the most inspiring role model for my life, was losing control of her entire body. We watched in disbelief, in awe, and sometimes in grief as she lost the ability to stand, to feed herself, to talk, and, finally, to move her diaphragm and breathe. She rarely cried, but tears streamed down her face when she realized she was losing her capacity to even talk. Total helplessness is such a difficult thing to watch, and the memory still brings tears to my eyes. Words cannot quite describe the feelings.

That is the nature of feelings sometimes, isn't it? Words don't always capture the experience, especially the intense emotions in all their power. All we can do is watch them and give ourselves compassion as the waves pass through us. In quietly sitting with them, becoming friends with the most heart-wrenching pain, we honor them. They just are what they are. Through honoring our emotions, we honor ourselves and others, because our emotions are a vital part of our life experience.

One of the ways I work with my emotions is to experience them as body states and then sit compassionately with those states, simply being with them. Over time I have befriended my emotions. They are no longer scary or intimidating. They just are, and now they are not overwhelming, though sometimes still intense. My feelings don't run the show, but are simply part of the life's palette of colors, fading in and out, sometimes in quiet tones, and other times with blinding shades of clashing colors as they move through my body.

Familiarity with this process of embracing emotion helped me manage the eighteen months of constant and unpredictable change with considerable equanimity. When one specialist did not return in the agreed-upon time frame to give us the results of a significant test, I calmly located her office in the hospital system and negotiated a timely consult. When there were some repeated miscommunications about one area of my mother's care, I calmly corrected them, several times, realigning the care with her needs. On one occasion my mother, totally out of character for her, snapped at me. I had informed the nurses about something minor that had been a problem, and it was immediately corrected. My mother did not like that I had told them and angrily snapped at me during a phone call. She was under incredible stress dealing with a condition that brought unimaginable pain and sorrow, and she had been showing magnificent resilience. When we could talk face-to-face, I let her know, with clarity and compassion, that I did not deserve being talked to that way, and I was only trying to help her. She apologized and never snapped at me again.

I was not always calm. I had returned home from the hospital after a long day, including receiving the diagnosis of ALS from my mother's physician. My mother was to be transferred to a nursing home in the next day or so, but we had not been informed of the specific date. She called me and said that the ambulance drivers had come to her room with the gurney to take her to the nursing home. I asked to talk with the staff and told the nurse that we had not been informed about this the entire day and that it needed to happen tomorrow. My voice had mild frustration in it, and I was definitely feeling this internally. She consulted with the resident who said my mother needed to go tonight. I raised my voice some and told her this was not acceptable, that I was exhausted, and they had not informed us earlier. She again consulted with the resident who said she had to go because it was "only 7:30" (at night). I responded, with irritation, trying to keep my calm as much as I could, that this would mean my coming to the hospital, then driving in the darkening unfamiliar roads to a place I had never been, helping her get settled, and dealing with the legal paperwork, maybe completing the process by 11pm. I asked to talk with the resident. She talked to him again, and graciously informed me that my mother could be transferred in the morning. The next morning I apologized to that nurse for my tone of voice, though not for my request. Were I to repeat this incident, I would have still insisted on a delayed transfer, but worked more with my internal state of frustration and irritation. We do our best with the emotions and keep going.

Another time of emotional upheaval came much earlier in that eighteen months, as my husband and I were preparing for the final move to the Louisville area. We had rented a moving truck which my husband was to drive. The movers arrived to fill it, and we discovered we had too much "stuff." I gave directions for what was optional and left to see clients for the last time. When I returned home, my husband had changed some of those directions, so some of the expected items were not on the truck. Frustration – getting on his case a little – not very mindful – and then recognition that I could innately trust my husband's intuition that I should no longer be climbing up on the 15 foot ladder to cut limbs off of trees and pick cherries, a beloved summer chore that gave us dried cherries all year. I let it go.

Then, as he was trying to jockey the truck in the driveway, I saw him backing up toward the garage. Fortunately, I could maintain my calm enough to not run behind the truck so he could see me waving my arms. I heard the crunch, and I must admit, I lost it, cursing once (not at him) and raising my voice for a few seconds. Why couldn't he pay attention! The walk-through for selling the house was in two days! Watching my emotions, I calmed down. I realized that my husband was so tired. He was doing the best he could, as was I, so I forgave myself for the outburst, apologized, and we went on – calmly. My mind, however, continued to chatter. What flashed through my head was the knowledge that it was only the gutter, but that gutter had been custom rolled because the roofer could not match the gutter color with what was readily available. How was this going to be repaired so the house could sell without further delay? Again I watched what I was doing internally and brought my mind back to the present. Just take the next step. My mind calmed some. I called my handyman, and he amazed me with his creativity, buying stock parts and using spray paint. It looked great when he was finished. Was I nervous during the process? A little, but it was manageable. And the house closed, but only after another delay from the buyer's mortgage company at the last minute. Life is often like this, isn't it? One more thing – usually unexpected – that we must manage in some semblance of calm.

THE BROADER PERSPECTIVE

Mindful Equanimity is a major factor in Mindful Resilience. Without it, emotions deplete your energy, distract you when you try to solve problems, and generally place obstacles of illogic in the midst of already challenging events. Like children, emotions are wonderful and normal, but they cannot be allowed to "run the show." Instead, listen to them as you would the children, upset as they might be, honoring the experience as it is and embracing them. Yes, I believe you can embrace your own process as you would embrace a child. And, like a child, the emotions usually calm, at least some, when heard and appreciated.

Working with emotions is about working with perspective. Mindfulness teaches you to observe while being with something: the breath, the mind, washing the dishes, or the internal states called emotions. Observing changes the way you look at the world and, thus, its impact on you.

Working mindfully with emotions is part of walking the path of the labyrinth. It impacts how you walk it. Being more present with your emotions allows you to more fully take in the other aspects of the journey, including those who are walking that same labyrinth. How do you feel when others are approaching you or when they pass by you without eye contact? How you internally handle those emotions impacts how you interact with others on the path. The more you are able to sit with and notice your emotional states, rather than just react to them, the easier it is to consciously choose your responses to whatever comes your way.

Developing Mindful Equanimity is a significant commitment, and one that may require therapy as well. If so, try to seek it out as a helpful adjunct. Whether with or without a therapist, a commitment to the process of befriending emotions takes you closer to yourself and to the world that greets you each day. Emotions are your friends and an incredible part of being human. In greeting them with compassion, you find the depth they can contribute to your life.

QUESTIONS YOU MIGHT CONSIDER

❋ What do you believe about emotions? How useful are these beliefs?

❋ What emotions are you most aware of as you face the current stress in your life?

❋ What are your patterns for dealing with strong emotions? How do these patterns work for you?

❋ What emotions are more comfortable for you and which less comfortable?

❋ Have you ever had the experience of having an emotion, being fully present with it, and yet a kind of calm about having it? What was that like?

MINDFUL EQUANIMITY EXERCISES:

EMOTION LOG: During one day, keep a log of each emotion you have as it arises and notice how you relate to it. You might push it away, distract yourself, notice it, or try to make it change. Just notice this with curiosity and without judgment. Know that you are doing your best with what you know now.

PEACEFUL ARRIVAL: When you are the most peaceful internally, how do you arrive at that place? Notice how this happens. Notice how this awareness then impacts your life.

EMOTION OBSERVATION: Pick an emotion that is mildly upsetting and watch it like you would watch a sunset or sunrise and notice any changes. Be curious. Working with emotions is an essential part of resiliency, and increased comfort with this part of you is well worth your time.

Chapter 11:
MINDFUL EMBODIMENT

Mindful Embodiment is a sense of trusting the process, of seeing and feeling the perfection in the moment. It feels like having the process move toward you as much as you are moving along the path. At its best, I believe it is similar to the process of flow described by Mihaly Csikszentmihalyi in his book *Flow: The Psychology of Optimal Experience.* For Csikszentmihalyi, flow is an internal experience when a person is totally in the present, challenged to live to the limit of his or her capacity but not beyond. The chosen activity is done for the sake of doing the activity, though the initial reasons motivating the activity may have been external. Activities, such as a job or a stressful experience, can be transformed so that the resulting experience is flow. The total engagement leads to a sense of being out of time, feeling in control of one's actions, and experiencing a sense of "flow" with life.[1]

This description of flow parallels my internal experience, at least to some degree. During my mother's illness, I often felt as if I were living outside of time. Although I certainly did not feel in control of the events unfolding in front of me, I did feel in control of my actions. Once my values were clear and major decisions made, the process seemed to move itself. This flow experience became greater as I moved farther along the path and spent more time being mindfully present with the process. I made decisions, but felt a part of the process, flowing with something larger than myself, rather than standing outside of the experience trying to figure it out. I danced, engaging the different rhythms of the events and challenges, changing my steps and adjusting as the dance floor shifted on its axis, with new partners of different skill levels and vastly different styles.

Experiences normally considered contradictory and mutually exclusive came together. I was both exhausted and enlivened, sad as I saw my mother decline and grateful to be sharing this emotionally intimate time with her. I felt helpless as I saw her life slip away and a sense of "rightness" that the timing of several decisions had allowed me this opportunity to help her. My emotions tasted like sugared ginger, a mix of sweet and sharp, combining to create its own distinctive, and intense, flavor.

In this process of Mindful Embodiment, when we act in ways that fully engage the moment, the moment − life itself − engages in return − life dancing as our partner, flowing with the moment in ways that look like miracles. There is a gratefulness of heart that seems to arise when we allow the moment to be most present, and to choose to be present in that moment. My heart became more open, both to life and to the depth of the moment, appreciating small things I might otherwise have missed. Being present helped me to both see them and appreciate them. The more skeptical person might have called them "serendipitous experiences," but we preferred to call them "miracles."[2]

"Miracles" often come from compassionate people willing to take the extra time. A few days after the bath experience, Mom fell on her way to the bathroom in the middle of the night. I flew out of bed and found her sprawled on the floor. She acknowledged she slipped but insisted she was fine. After resting a minute, still on the floor, she wanted to stand, claiming to be in no pain. "I'm fine." The next morning she described the pain as mild and did not want to see a doctor. As the pain increased, I insisted on medical care, and she agreed to be seen at a clinic. The physician there suspected a spinal fracture and told us to go to an emergency room, but he refused to give us any guidance in choosing the best medical facility for her condition, apparently following clinic rules. A complete stranger in the waiting room, a physical therapy student who knew the hospitals in the area, told us which hospital was known for its specialty in treating spine issues. We chose that hospital's emergency room. Many hours later, Mom was fitted with a back brace that looked like, and apparently felt like, a compression version of a torture rack. Late that evening, they sent us home.

The back brace was excruciating for her, and the brace specialist had offered to adjust it if needed. We were in his office the next day. He could lift and move her in ways that minimized her significant pain, and he adjusted the brace. As we were leaving, he offered to assist us, at no extra charge, to take the brace on and off as needed, every few days if necessary. He was burly, quite a contrast to my petite frame, and I was grateful. Just helping her move around at this point was quite a chore.

The fracture and the brace brought a lot of pain, so she refused to lie down. When her legs began to swell, I decided we needed to return to the emergency room. But that was not the main problem. On the way out of my house, her legs totally collapsed as she slowly made her way down the three stairs toward my car. Fortunately, I had been purposely walking behind her and caught her fall onto my body. We barely made it to the car. When I arrived at the emergency room and brought the wheel chair out to the car, I stood there for a minute. Now what do I do? Out of the corner of my eye, I saw an emergency technician, another burly guy, walking toward his ambulance. He must have seen the look on my face, came over to the car, and literally lifted her into the wheel chair. With tears in my eyes, I thanked him for his great kindness.

This kind of help happened on other occasions. The office assistant who was "not supposed to help" guided my mother's body and acted as a back-up for me as I slid my mother along the sliding board from car to wheel chair and, later, back the other direction. The security woman at the mall assisted me with the sliding board and helped me lift Mom into and out of an optometrist chair so she could see again with stronger glasses. Now she could enjoy her computer (for a short period) and read, a great joy for her. The small things counted so much. Total strangers made me feel like we were cared for.

The nursing home, aptly named "The Taj Mahal" by the nursing staff who worked there, was another miracle. The large single rooms were tastefully decorated, with space for family to live alongside the resident if needed, and I found it inviting and enjoyable. There was a large fish tank, an aviary, excellent food, terrific PT and OT staff, and excellent nursing care. The physician attending to my mother was excellent, reviewing and selectively reducing the numerous medications prescribed at the hospital before I even had to ask. She was attentive to my mother's changing needs and coordinated treatment with my mother's neurologist.

We didn't "find" this place; it "found" us. The hospital gave us a couple of days notice before she had to be released, and I had no idea what nursing homes were good and no time to visit them. We were still talking to doctors about the cause of her growing weakness, and diagnostic tests were not yet complete. I hoped for the branch of the rehabilitation center where she had initially received excellent care, a branch close to my home. This center's representative informed us that my mother was not appropriate for their facility because she needed more care than they could provide. After hearing this, I followed that representative out the door and asked what nursing homes had good reputations. She said she could not tell me. This was another of those less-than-helpful-follow-the-rules decisions, but I wasn't taking "no" for an answer.

I explained our situation and that we didn't know what was available since I had just moved to the area. Graciously, she went through the nursing home guidebook, pointing out some nursing homes with good reputations. I then worked with the social worker and chose two facilities that would send representatives for a visit. One of the representatives said my mother "was accepted." The other representative looked at her and said, "We want you to come." I was amazed since her primary neurologist had just prescribed a very expensive medication for her ALS, and I had learned by that point that the nursing home had to pick up the cost of what was not covered by Medicare and her supplemental insurance. Also, since they only had private rooms, Medicare would cover that cost. Without visiting, we chose this one and never regretted it. What a gift! The level of support provided by our "Taj Mahal" made the process manageable, and I am forever grateful for everyone who helped make those last few very difficult months as easy and enjoyable as possible.

The motorized recliner was another gift. Because of her ALS, my mother no longer had the padding needed for basic comfort in bed, and she was frequently in considerable discomfort, and sometimes pain. At this point she could no longer move herself, and the nursing aides were wonderful with the frequent repositioning needed. One of the aides mentioned the idea of a motorized recliner which would expand her positioning options. When I asked whether I could see one on the floor, she obtained permission from another patient, and I walked in to see an extremely plump pink chair that came alive with the push of a button. As I thanked my mother's neighbor for allowing me to see her chair, she informed me that this chair was 10 days old, did not fit her needs, and was for sale. I arranged for my mother to try the chair, and she loved it. She nodded, smiled widely, and her eyes danced like those of a happy child. We bought it, the maintenance men moved it across the hall, and it was hers. This "miracle" chair was invaluable in giving her comfort during the last weeks of her life. She could be moved from bed to chair, and both devices could also be adjusted. The aides, with the help of sometimes a dozen pillows, graciously adjusted her body at all hours. In that chair, she could also smell the cool breeze from the nearby window, tasting the outdoors, even into November. What a gift. I periodically think of that pink recliner and the comfort it brought her – and continues to bring – as it makes its way from patient to patient in that home.

There were other small miracles that make me smile. Fruit juice was served on the unit each afternoon, and both Mother and I loved the grape juice. One day, the grape juice wasn't offered as an option. I contacted the kitchen and was told they were not buying it anymore. I am a persistent person and asked another person on another day, and received the same answer. Then grape juice appeared in the afternoons again, unrequested. We enjoyed it until she died. I am also curious, and I asked again, after the grape juice began to appear without request, whether they had grape juice, and I was again told they had stopped buying grape juice. Amazing! We simply smiled, enjoyed it, and called it a miracle.

An administrative staff person provided notary service when we needed it. On one occasion, we needed something to be notarized with an embossed notary stamp which the staff person did not have. When I asked if someone else could meet this need, I found that such a person had just started working at the nursing home – that day. Of course. We just smiled.

I look back at that time with tears and smiles, so much pain and so many gifts. It was like life was making as much of an effort as we were to embody the present with its hopelessness and its awe, with its withholdings and with its abundance. It was beautiful in an odd way, just as a weather-exposed tree is beautiful with its distorted branches and cracked bark, or a broken conch shell with weather-worn edges.

Fully being with the tree or listening to the shell offers whispers of something beyond who we are, beyond what we see and do, giving us a taste of the Greater that can never be earned, but is only savored as the blessed gift that it is.

THE BROADER PERSPECTIVE

At this point, you are in the flow of walking the labyrinth. The labyrinth is your life at that moment, and you are engrossed in the experience. Time may feel suspended as you go deeper into the experience, but you are totally present with what is in front of you. Life can have this flow to it, maybe especially in challenging times because it pushes you to the edge of your abilities. Moving into the flow of an experience seems to engage life in a special way.

Wonderful, sometimes seemingly miraculous experiences are part of life, even in challenging times. It requires being present in the moment to see them. Being grateful for these moments seems to bring more. An appreciative attitude contributes to other people's innate desire to be helpful. There are other contributing factors as well. You may be afraid to allow joy to touch your heart when the next moment or the next day you fear having to grieve again or deal with a new challenge. That is understandable, and you can decide how much you are ready to face.

I invite you to engage this flow experience as a way of engaging life more. It is a way to move with the river of life, taste its flavors, and experience its awe. This flow and its gifts are there all the time for us to experience. Being challenged seems to make this experience more accessible. The dying experience is especially suited to facilitating this work, with its subtle and profound moments, but you can engage life and find its flow in any situation. Simply begin with what you are facing now.

QUESTIONS YOU MIGHT CONSIDER

❋ Remember a time when you felt in the flow of life, totally involved with what was in front of you. What allowed you to go there?

❋ What gifts does this moment, right now, have for you?

❋ What inspired awe in you today?

❋ Do you regularly look for "miracles?" If not, why not?

❋ When was the last time you gave the gift of "a miracle" to another person?

MINDFUL EMBODIMENT EXERCISES:

AN AWE-FILLED MOMENT: What brings you a feeling of awe? You may relate to being in nature, watching a child play, or watching a sunset. Decide what would be a good match for you and create this experience for yourself. In other words, take the time to actually do it – watch the child or the sunset. While you are doing this, notice how you feel inside and just be with that state, noticing it. Notice how this impacts your day.

A GRATEFUL MOMENT: Think of a current life challenge. Now think of something related to this experience that has been helpful to you. Allow yourself to feel grateful for this helpful aspect, going inside and being appreciative. Now notice what happens to your perspective of the challenge.

A MIRACLE GIVEN: Think of someone who is feeling challenged in their life. Be creative and think of some small way you can help them, whether it is doing something nice for them or letting them know you are thinking of them. Now carry this through. You can decide whether you tell them it was from you. How do you feel internally after giving this gift? Does this change how you feel about your own life challenge?

Heart-Based Relating Along the Path

As we walk the labyrinth's path, we may choose connection with others. Compassion allows us to connect in a way that is respectful for each of those concerned when we allow the depth, timing, and intensity to match the situation. Compassion moves outward toward the other as well as inward, as we find a balance between our own needs and the needs of those we meet. How do we relate in a way that most fully respects the needs of all concerned?

In life, relating to others is not optional. Developing the capacity for compassion is important because it is compassion that leads us to connection, especially at the deeper levels of connection where we touch others' vulnerability as well as our own. We also need to have compassion toward ourselves and balance our own lives, particularly when we face challenges. It is essential that we balance our own needs and the needs of others, especially those who depend on our care. This heart-based attitude encircles all concerned in a gentleness that is so necessary when we are dealing with complex decision-making and a cacophony of emotions. Compassion offers a kind of holding, adding to the Mindful Embracing a gentleness of spirit and emotional respite, making a place for your own weariness or that of another to be heard, and the human spirit restored.

Chapter 12:
MINDFUL COMPASSION-TO-CONNECTION

Compassion is the doorway to connection, in both giving and receiving. Mindful Compassion-to-Connection describes a conscious creating in both directions, choosing and walking the path of compassion, moving toward others and allowing them to move toward us. In compassion, the essence of two beings touch, both appreciating their essential connection, and at the same time maintaining the integrity of separateness.

The challenges I have written about offered opportunity to grow in this area. For many years, my professional work brought me in contact with people going through hard times. Even if I did not support their actions, I found that there were always reasons why they acted as they did. Being compassionate is more challenging when we are asked to give things up. Compassion for my husband's discomfort was a challenge because it directly impacted our decision about where to live, requiring me to face several significant losses. Surrender was needed, making smooth the rough edges and fine tuning the heart. Allowing ourselves to be touched may feel risky, and opening in this way can lead to interesting adventures and unknown places. What we are guaranteed is growth along the way. Once I allowed compassion to lead, life became both more challenging and more interesting.

When we choose compassion, the underground river of life seems to move things along. Once moving, compassion flows more easily. How could I not be compassionate with my mother's medical situation? ALS is relentless in the progressive loss of function and in the increasing helplessness of the patient, the caregiver and the family. Allowing myself to ride the depth of that process with her as much as I could meant I had to let myself be in contact with those feelings.

I watched the swallow study as they put a tube down her throat and saw how much this basic survival process was affected. I watched how hard she tried in OT and PT, striving to improve when the ALS was constantly pulling in the opposite direction. I watched as mild electric shocks were used by the OT and speech therapists to stimulate the muscles, with some success, and at times considerable discomfort. I helped transfer her from the bed to a chair or wheelchair, sometimes using the Hoyer lift, and I helped feed her and interpret her speech.

I felt one of my jobs was to understand what she was experiencing so I could make sure she received the best care possible. I made the choice to "get it" as much as anyone can understand what it is like to be another person. My compassion for her increased as I watched her experience these aspects of her medical care and assisted in her care as needed. Twice I awakened from dreams of having difficulty swallowing and limited movement in my body, a terrifying experience and probably close to Mom's reality. Of course my imagining myself in her body was not the same as actually experiencing it nor anywhere near as difficult as her experience. Compassion can help us touch another's experience, and this can lead to a profound sense of connection.

Choose the level of connection that is right for you and your situation. I chose this level of intensity because I wanted to fully experience my mother's transition and to be deeply present with her in the sunset of her life. I had the luxury of a husband who could financially support me, and many people giving support and assistance, allowing me the opportunity to spend many hours with her. Because Mom was given up by her biological parents at a young age and adopted by my grandmother, she had always feared being abandoned. I was determined she would not experience abandonment again if I could help it. I loved her deeply and cherished this deep sharing of her life. This choice helped me expand and deepen my capacity for love and sharing, aspects of myself I had chosen to grow over the years. It was an opportunity that would come only once, and I am glad I chose to really be present in it with her.

I received as well as gave. I was blessed to have several levels of support, despite having just arrived in the community when my mother entered the hospital system, and her care and needs became my top priority. She herself was supportive which may be unusual. We nurtured our relationship over the years with regular phone calls and visits. We reached out to each other. I traveled to visit her, and she traveled to visit me. We had become very good friends, and that bond allowed for frank sharing, compassionate words, and many times just being together without words, sometimes sitting side by side, while at other times holding her in the hospital bed.

I was also blessed to have a loving husband who, despite having spent months apart with only visits, totally supported my spending hours and then weeks with her. He was open to listening and sharing, and his own loving compassion carried me through many of the times that seemed too sad and heavy to bear. My sisters were also incredible, driving or flying many miles to come and relieve me so I could have minor surgery myself or just rest. They were ready to listen on the phone to my feelings and concerns, both before and after her death, and we all became closer during this process. My father's second wife, who had so recently lost her own husband, was incredibly supportive. She drove to meet me half-way, bringing food and other items that could be helpful. She later sent cooked food by others so that I had less cooking to do. And she totally supported the focus on my mother when she would have enjoyed time with me herself.

I recognize that I am remarkably blessed with my family members. Many people have family members who seem uninterested, uncaring, or caustic, or have disappeared altogether. My heart always feels sad hearing about those situations since I know what family support can be like. Perhaps there is one family member who can be supportive. Take advantage of what you do have and nurture it, for it is a gem.

Beyond family, friends and even neighbors can offer support. Two neighbors brought us cooked meals once they heard that my mother was so ill. I was incredibly touched by their thoughtfulness. Friends from Chicago called periodically, often just leaving messages because I was frequently unavailable to speak with them – or sent e-mails – inquiring about how things were going. Even though I rarely talked directly to them, I felt their presence as a powerful support because I knew they were thinking about me and told them so later. And then there was Muffy, a woman I met at a farmer's market the first week or two after arriving in town. We had met a couple of times for coffee before Mom's arrival, and then I was unavailable. She came to visit my mother and me at the nursing home, bless her. I am so grateful. She invited my husband and myself to Thanksgiving, just days after my mother's death. She and her family were so thoughtful, and I will always remember her expression of compassion.

My church was also an important source of support. The first Sunday I attended services early in my mother's illness, I asked them to pray for her. They prayed for her that day and, despite my irregular attendance, they continued to do so until she died. The pastor visited the nursing home bringing communion for both of us, a touching experience. For many months following her death, several women would regularly come up to me at church and ask how I was doing. I had been cared about and prayed for despite being a total stranger.

Nor should we forget support groups. I went only once to a caregiver's support group, but it was an important aspect of my support. Even a single contact can help. At the group, I obtained much information that was helpful as I moved forward. I also knew that I could return and find listening ears and compassion if I needed them. The ALS Association was very helpful, providing information on the illness and caretaking options. Though I never attended an ALS support group meeting, I knew it was available and likely would have attended had my mother's illness been more extended. Hospice was also invaluable in their emotional support as well as information regarding options of care for both my mother and my father.

The nursing home staff was very supportive. Because I spent so much time there, and lived with her as she neared the end of her life, I knew many of the employees by name. They became another community of support, so touched by my mother that they had their own memorial service for her when she died. People had grown to love her and, bless them, told her so. My mother was an incredible "old soul" (as my youngest sister called her), and she asked her care-givers about their lives and told them she loved them. And, they responded − in kind.

I was so grateful for the support around me and let it nurture me. Many bonds grew, some temporary, while others enhanced already close relationships. For everyone, I think this type of compassion builds the capacity to give and receive love, a valuable resource as we walk further into life. I am grateful for all I was given.

Through it all I gained a greater appreciation of the capacity to love. Nothing is more courageous than daring to love, whether we open our heart to ourselves, to others, or to whatever we experience as Spirit. No matter how much love we give, it remains available when we want to give again. Love, at its highest, is selfless and genuine, deep and upward-spirited, with a perfume and essence that lingers in the air, falling gently on all in its presence. It touches hearts and minds, breathes hope into hopelessness, and fosters connection in the midst of alienation. Love, not ego, must lead the act of compassion in order for its ephemeral quality to enliven, for ego only makes for theatre. There is humility in loving that reflects awe, for in loving we perceive a connection to the Divine in life – self or other it matters not, for loving one truly is loving the other. Are we not all one?

THE BROADER PERSPECTIVE

Compassion-to-Connection is how you move into compassion for yourself and others and, from this place of understanding, moving toward the level of connection you choose with those around you. This requires appreciating both your own situation and those with whom you interact. Building skills of compassion and empathy is a process that takes time.

Mindfulness embraces the non-judgment of self and others that provides the foundation for this process. It can help you shift perspective and notice what you see when you simply observe. It is the intention for compassion and empathy that is important. Nobody is perfect in their understanding. It is the moving in that direction that changes the tone in relationships and facilitates increased connection.

Remember that neither empathy nor compassion requires agreement. You can appreciate that someone is in great pain about their life situation and also know that you do not deserve the screaming directed at you. In this and all situations, you can also have compassion for yourself. If you choose a position of less connection, it is possible to consciously create this distance while maintaining compassion for both yourself and the other person. My philosophy is that each person is doing their best with what they have and what they know at the time. It is your right to choose what kinds of interactions you allow in your life.

Compassion-to-Connection in the labyrinth walk includes all of the opportunities that come when you pass, are passed by, or walk close to another person in the labyrinth. It might also be your connection with them when you see them at another location. You can choose to make eye contact, smile, or maintain your inner focus on your path. The choice is yours alone, maintaining the mindful perspective of observing the interaction as well as the non-judging attitude about the entire process and your choice in how you handle it.

How different life would be if everyone were compassionate toward everyone else. That process begins with you – and with me. May we all find that path.

QUESTIONS YOU MIGHT CONSIDER

❋ Think of a challenging situation for you and the main person you must interact with in that situation. What can you appreciate about the pain (physical and non-physical) they seem to be experiencing?

❋ How connected are you to that person? How do you help maintain that level of connection or disconnection?

❋ What level of connection would be respectful to both of you?

❋ How do you need to change your interactions with that person to develop the level of connection you want to have? (Note that you may want more disconnection, and this may mean putting up boundaries. The concept of connection is a continuum.)

MINDFUL CONNECTION-TO-COMPASSION EXERCISES

COMPASSION WITH ANOTHER: Bring to mind someone (or an animal) you care about and with whom you have a positive relationship. Think about a challenging time for them. Now allow yourself to care about what they feel or felt and feel a little of it yourself. What is that like for you? What do you learn about yourself?

COMPASSION WITH A MORE CHALLENGING OTHER: Think of someone whom you experience as mildly difficult. Notice how you feel in your body. Consider the idea that each person has a story, and each person is struggling to survive the best way they know how. You don't have to choose to be their friend, or even be around them, but they have a story just like you. See them in front of you. Just notice them as another human being who has hurts and disappointments, a fellow traveler on planet earth with all of its challenges. Now again notice how you feel inside your body. How has your own experience of them and of yourself changed as you are able to feel empathy towards them?

RECEIVING CONNECTION (PART A): Sit quietly with yourself and ask yourself whether you are feeling enough support at the moment. If yes, is it the kind you need? If no, what kind do you need? Do you need someone to listen? Or do you need to interact in a more playful way with someone, to laugh, or to have a deep conversation? Once you identify this, what is the fist step toward finding this? If you need to develop friends, this will take time. Support groups are available for many areas of concern and a useful place to start. The important thing is to move in the direction that is meaningful for you. Maybe you simply need to call someone you know. Developing a support system is a process and one that requires dedication (remember the Commitment-to-Transformation?). Be patient and keep the process going.

RECEIVING CONNECTION (PART B): Once you have any opportunity to receive what you have identified, be fully present as you experience the presence of that support. This can be very hard. Just do your best. If you need to pull back, do so. Take it at your pace. We all assume this is easy, but that is not so for everyone. Now savor what you allowed yourself to experience.

COMPASSION FOR YOURSELF: This area is the most challenging one for many people. Again, find a quiet time and place. Consider a time you went through that was challenging. Just appreciate the impact on you and your life, the challenges, and how you coped (no, not perfectly, but that is never the point). You did the best you could with what you had. Care about yourself in that experience. Embrace yourself with compassion. You may not be able to fully embrace yourself at first. Have compassion for yourself as you recall this challenge. We all had different life experiences and thus, different skills. Be kind to yourself along this path.

Chapter 13:

MINDFUL AWARENESS-TO-BALANCE

Mindful-Awareness-to-Balance is being present with the different aspects of life and our sense of their relative balance or imbalance, then using that awareness to create the balance in our life that is best for us. Physical well-being, social support, mental aliveness, alignment with values, and connection to Spirit are all areas to consider. How to balance our time among these parts of life is the question. Are any particularly neglected? If so, what is the most effective way to rebalance the life system?

I maintained my balance more easily while I was living in Chicago. When I would visit my husband, he and I enjoyed time with each other, walking, talking, and sitting in quiet. He and my mother were my best friends. I also spoke with her regularly, which I always found a joy. I made time to be in Mississippi for her 82nd birthday, unaware that it would be her last.

After choosing to move, I continued to see my friends whenever I could, keeping up with them and not just saying goodbye. Seeing clients in my clinical practice continued to bring me joy and was part of my balance. Even the office staff brought smiles to my face and ease to my life as we negotiated my seeing some clients there when in town after the move. I sat with Spirit, sometimes talking, mostly trying to be receptive. I easily found connection with Spirit in my backyard's natural beauty, especially in winter when deep snows enfolded those moments in a soft stillness. I took my time and packed in stages.

The balance started to unravel after my husband moved and I was well into the packing. I lifted things I should not have lifted. I told myself that "someone had to do it." That may have been true, but in retrospect it did not have to be me. I hired people to do some things, but I could have enlisted or purchased more help than I did. I was not mindful of my body's capacity and needs, and the old thought, "There is so much to do" prevailed. I pushed my body beyond its limit because of this lack of awareness.

I drove to southern Indiana repeatedly to see both my father and my husband. The drives added to my stress, but I balanced the physical cost against the need to maintain my connection with those I loved by being physically present with them, and I would not choose otherwise were I to choose again. Mostly, however, I followed a pace that was not exhausting.

Near the end of the Chicago experience, I began to push, pulling a full trailer to Indiana in pouring rain and moving too many things myself. I made choices out of balance with my needs. I thought I would make the final move and be able to slow down for a few months, slowly unpacking. I expected that I could take some time off and catch up on rest and sleep. That assumption was a mistake.

I didn't count on escorting and guiding my mother through hospital forays and medical adventures. Already tired, I allowed this new challenge to push me off balance, so I didn't stay aware of my own needs. I simply put her first. Making her a priority was the right thing, but I did not keep track fully of what I needed as well. And I forgot to mention that I made three trips to Chicago for oral surgery after Mom's hospitalization, while my middle sister watched over her care. I could have chosen otherwise, but I was not attentive to my own level of exhaustion. I just pushed forward. For several months, I continued to sleep at home every night, visiting her during the day, and then every other day as I felt the fatigue. Then I decided that someone needed to be with her all of the time.

Packing a suitcase, I moved into her room. I took breaks by walking outside among trees, walking laps in the nursing home halls late at night, or making phone calls, but was basically by her side on call "24/7." I offered an extra pair of hands to care for her needs and was there to interpret what she was trying to say as she lost the ability to speak clearly or above a faint whisper, and these tasks often came in the middle of the night. I rubbed her now uncomfortable and painful legs and washed her face with a warm washcloth, feeling privileged to participate in her few remaining pleasures as the weeks brought total paralysis.

About a week before she died, before my younger sister arrived for a second time to help, I simply had to go home from my 24-hour watch to sleep in my own bed. When I lay down, I was surprised how much my entire body hurt. Shocked by my level of exhaustion, I woke up to the bigger picture. Though I returned to living with her the few days until my sister arrived, I let my loving sister take over at that point, and I slept at home. That decision was a hard one for me because I wanted to be present at her moment of death. I missed that moment, but I think that's what my mother had in mind, for it seems she died with nobody in the room, independent spirit that she was.

The imbalance was in my inattention to my own physical needs. I was getting mentally challenged and stimulated by the decisions that had to be made. My social support was great. I took time for Spirit, in quiet attunement and prayer, and in being with her, which felt like a calling at that point. I ate fairly well, finishing her food but also eating the nutritious food that my husband brought on several occasions. The problem was my mounting exhaustion that remained outside of my awareness.

How could I have maintained better balance for my physical needs? Looking back, I could have been more aware of my tiredness level. That awareness would have prompted me to explore other options. It is amazing how much the lens of perception shapes the moment. Had I chosen to put on different lenses, other options would have "emerged," clear now in the new light. I was surprised that the need for physical self care could be so overlooked. I was blessed that others were there to help, and that the nursing home, in addition to providing excellent care for my mother, also allowed me to come and go as I as needed. We anticipated that we might have her in my home, but that did not happen. How long could I have maintained caring for her at home, despite my deep love for her? Seeing my limitations, I investigated other options, but she died before that challenge arose.

Then I could rest. It has been almost a year since her death, and I can see the consequences of my exhaustion. I need extra sleep just to feel rested. I miss Mom, but I am happy with my life and want to do more. Patience, I remind myself, patience is needed here. I also have trigger finger, an inflammation in my hand, probably a consequence of over-use during the moving and her physical care, and now there is time to deal with that. So I am making up for the pushing I did and only now starting to do serious exercise again. Now I seek not to lose touch with that need for rest and sleep – and simply stop when pressures mount and life issues become demanding. Some things have to be done, but there are always choices. I intend to stay more in touch with my own physical needs so that this part of me does not become depleted.

THE BROADER PERSPECTIVE

Mindful Awareness-to-Balance requires you to broaden your perspective by putting the wide angle lens on your camera. What is in front of you is your life, all aspects of it at once. It is becoming aware of how it all fits together – or not, with some parts of your life possibly crying out for attention. Taking in this broad range may be a lot to expect, but the inattention often means we have to correct the balance later.

Your imbalance may or may not be neglecting your physical limitations. Maybe you are allowing others to berate you or allowing your work to engage you so much that you lose connections with people who are important to you. Whatever your imbalance, bring mindfulness and its tenant of non-judging to the task of understanding. Just notice what you are doing, being present with it.

Learning this process and becoming more able to balance it is part of the journey as well. Nobody is perfect, myself included. The work is to notice your patterns and your choices, make new decisions, and keep learning. The beauty is in the unfolding.

QUESTIONS YOU MIGHT CONSIDER

�֍ Where is your life in balance?

✖ Where is your life out of balance?

✖ What perspective or expectations of yourself do you have about different aspects of your life that seems to be unbalancing that system?

✖ How might you change that perspective?

✖ What kind of checking in do you need to do so that you maintain the balance best for you?

MINDFUL AWARENESS-TO-BALANCE
EXERCISES

BECOMING AWARE OF IMBALANCE: Sit quietly and bring attention to the three large life areas of mind, body, and spirit. What do you notice first? Does your connection to Spirit need attention? Is your body calling for exercise and movement? Are your emotions craving to be heard? Does your mind want some stimulation? Does another area call to you? Identify the area. If clarity does not come when sitting, just allow this question to remain and revisit it during the day until something comes.

WHAT BALANCE WOULD LOOK LIKE: Once you have identified the area, sit quietly and listen for how your body and self want to move into balance. This instruction may sound vague; yet see if you can let the answer come into your mind from the process of just noticing. One thing I have learned about people is that they know more than they think they do about themselves, if they learn to listen quietly and deeply.

MOVING INTO BALANCE: Now, implement the insight. Again, listen and respect the pace your body needs. Act, and watch – notice. When I started an exercise video, I noticed my right knee was feeling some strain, so I decided to warm up my knees before doing the tape. What does your body, mind, or spirit say to you as you proceed? Listen, and shift. This is resilience at the micro level.

Reaching Into the Depth and Center of the Labyrinth

The labyrinth leads us gradually toward the center and, metaphorically, toward the center of our lives and ourselves. We can think of this as our Wisdom Center, the place of greatest depth in ourselves. From this place comes a knowingness of the best of who we can be as well as the clearest intent to move in that direction. This is a process of refining ourselves which moves us deeper and closer to our highest potential of who we are. This Mindful Refinement of ourselves and Mindful Attunement to the Wisdom Center seem to go hand in hand, with the work of each supporting the other. The center is not a stagnant place, but a place of knowing to which we return. Returning, learning can deepen, and wisdom can grow. And we move deeper still, bringing our fullest self forward as a gift to the world.

Chapter 14:
MINDFUL REFINEMENT

Why bother with life, especially when it seems so difficult at times – or even all the time? Only in being present can we become the greatest version of ourselves possible – only by committing to really live, can we expand into our highest potential. I am sitting outside writing on a cloudless day in early November, surrounded by leafless trees and budding shrubs, with the warmth of the sun on my face. It would be a rare day back in my old home in Chicago when I could enjoy sitting outside in November. But I've moved to a new land! And we can live in a new way as well, with warmth and light shining on and through us even in the harshest of life's seasons. Like the sun, we give to others. Our highest potential shines forth as an offering of service to make the world a better place. In turn, we receive from those who can give something back. We also receive in the experience of giving when we work with those who cannot reciprocate. Living this way, we find the best in ourselves, whatever that is, and then radiate that gift into the lives of others.

Mindful Refinement is consciously choosing action that facilitates this process of development, integrating our innate gifts with the work where we find the greatest joy. We seek to align our actions and circumstances with our life purpose, using our capacity fully, growing in the direction that feels joyous and fulfilling. This way of living often means learning new skills in addition to building on what we already have.

Writing this book is part of my own process of Mindful Refinement. My inner voice whispered for years about working with resilience, and the voice became louder as time and events proceeded. Being mindfully present to that inner voice and responding to it was long in coming, but now I am finally writing. Writing has been a way to clarify what I learned in this set of challenges and to develop some new skills in my own life as I write and publish this material. I cannot know what impact this book will have on others' lives, yet following the call to move forward, not knowing, is surely part of the journey of refinement for me, like walking into the unknown of the move to my new home and into the unknown of ALS with my mother.

Other voices arise inside: "What if I fail?" Then I ask myself, what would "failure" be? That other people don't find this useful? Some people will not find it fits their needs, but some people probably will. If I do not try by publishing the work and seeing the responses, I will never know. In the act of writing I have also clarified things for myself, honoring my experience and finding a language that is meaningful for me in my life.

Resilience includes moving forward after the challenging events are over. What comes after the lesson is clarifying what was learned, appreciating that even more change may be needed, and moving forward, again into the unknown. In this way, Mindful Refinement happens both during and between challenges. It is an ongoing process of being ever open to opportunity. For example, while attending the celebration of my mother's life, a friend of hers asked me about my career plans. When I shared that I was interested in the field of resilience, she told me that a workshop on resilience was being offered the next week in a nearby community – and it was free. Coincidence? Unable to reach the sponsors to ask about participation, I nevertheless arranged my schedule to attend. Then I reached the workshop organizer and confirmed my registration.

Mindful Refinement includes following the lead of our hearts and minds. When we do, some doors will open. Some doors will close, and that is a message too. Then we keep going, learning from all that happens. The process is not always easy, but it is an adventure, and it can happen in our own backyard.

THE BROADER PERSPECTIVE

You are in process of refining yourself, and life's challenges are the greatest classrooms available to you. They smooth the edges of your personality, push you to reach deeply for your strengths and potential, and sometimes rip away roadblocks that have stood in your way for years. To gain the most, you need to be present as you look deeply for clarity and then spread your wings broadly to soar to your greatest heights. You are responsible for maintaining focus, continuing to move forward, and making the best choices you know how to make.

Mindful Refinement is moving into the center of the labyrinth. You are moving into the core of yourself, the best you can be in the moment. Being mindful and present in the process on the path has brought you forward to this place. Perfection is not found in some abstract or legalistic sense, but in perfect resonance with or attunement to the present moment, stepping forward and doing your best.

Mindful Refinement is not a goal but another process. Because life is always moving, completion continues to expand. It is your job to maintain mindful presence as best you can to further expand into your best self. Amazingly, your refinement process does not belong to you, but is an expansion into the world, and is integrated into the refining of everyone.

QUESTIONS YOU MIGHT CONSIDER

❋ Who are you at your very best? Where is that taking you, to your best understanding?

❋ What does your heart want you to explore in your life?

❋ What is the legacy you would like to leave for others you love?

❋ What is the legacy you would like to leave for the larger world community?

❋ What needs to happen in your life for you to feel complete?

MINDFUL REFINEMENT EXERCISES

DARE TO DREAM: What is the greatest and highest dream for your life? Let go – and dream. Take time and write in your journal. Just write without criticism and see what comes. No one else needs to read it, and your thoughts are not written in concrete. It can all change. What I discovered when I wrote without ongoing critique was that my writing had some surprises I probably would not have found had I focused on "quality" or "correctness." Whatever comes is fine. Even if you only receive hints, that is a start, for this is an exercise that can be repeated.

LIVING YOUR GREATEST POTENTIAL: What is the first step in moving toward your highest potential? Break things down until the first step becomes manageable. When I decided to write this book, I needed to make that goal manageable. To narrow the plan enough for me, I decided to write one page daily. Though I have not been entirely consistent, sometimes writing less and sometimes more, I made progress toward the goal of completing a book on resilience.

STEP INTO REFINEMENT: Now, schedule that first step. Yes, actually write down a date, and schedule a time. Now you have an appointment with yourself to start things rolling. Mindfully do that step, savoring the experience of stepping into your greatest potential.

Chapter 15:
MINDFUL ATTUNEMENT

Mindful Attunement is a more subtle concept and harder to put into words. Words are limited by their nature, yet they can serve as signposts on our journey. This process of Mindful Attunement moves us towards creating the fullest self discussed in the previous chapter. That fullest self is our destination, where we are going in our journey, both through and beyond times requiring great resilience. Mindful Attunement points us in that direction and seeks to engage us with something that pulls us forward.

Mindful Attunement seeks awareness of the depth or level of refinement we want to engage or embrace at any particular moment. In this process we choose to connect with and live in alignment with that deepest level. We move toward Mindful Attunement by feeling or sensing our depth. When we choose attunement with the deepest, most refined level of possibility in the moment, we find our deepest Inner Wisdom. This awareness is not an intellectual activity, but a felt sense of what is most holy in the moment. I use the word "holy" to point toward the very best of human possibility, to indicate something greater than who we perceive ourselves to be, a Self we can grow into if we choose to be guided by what I regard as our Inner Wisdom.

The source of that Inner Wisdom has been called different names by different people. I use the broad term "Spirit" in this book so that people using any of the names for Divine Presence might relate. Since words by their nature only symbolize aspects of actual experiences, all are inadequate. Some people reading this book will see Inner Wisdom as the best of being human, and I honor that as a legitimate way to use this material. Some people will relate these words to being beyond human.

For me, accessing Inner Wisdom comes from attuning with Spirit, becoming more like that Divine Essence, and attempting to do this on a moment-by-moment basis. That attunement then leads to different choices in my intent and behavior. I have described personal experiences that led me to perceive, touch, and feel something larger than myself during this personal journey. You might consider this Greater Reality to be external to yourself or within yourself. My experience tells me it is within us, and that going deeper into our experience moves us closer to that Reality.

My experience of God (one of my personal words for Spirit) seemed to change over the year and a half, especially in the last few months leading to my mother's death. Of course God didn't change; only my perspective changed. God seemed to become more expansive, more subtle, more intense, and more powerful. I believe that the aspects of Mindful Resilience, especially Mindful Embracing, facilitated this shift. It seemed that embracing each moment in all of its challenges with as much love and compassion as I could find within myself, led to embracing Spirit or God in a different way also. This experience then increased my attunement in the moment, aligning my choices with the best I had to offer.

I am incredibly grateful for this experience. It is a gift, not something I "earned." We all have the potential to have these kinds of experiences in our lives. I believe mindfulness and some of the concepts discussed in this book give us more access to this increased attunement with Spirit.

Mindful Attunement is more subtle than Mindful Alignment. Mindful Alignment can be clarified with thinking and then simply decided. In Mindful Attunement we move toward our greatest potential in the world and toward that greatest potential within, into the flow of what is known as opposed to believed, into a felt sense of knowing.

Belief can be challenged and shaken, knowing cannot. It is like a stream returning to the sea.

Attuning to Spirit within, accessing our deepest Inner Wisdom, reminds us that we are more than we seem to be. Remembering who we really are, not in the future, but right here and now, we attune ourselves to that Reality. This process is like tuning and playing a piano. Playing a note brings it into being. Each string is tuned to integrate harmoniously with the other strings. When played by a skilled pianist, the piano becomes greater than its individual strings, capable of bringing tears to the eye and making hearts sing. When we attune ourselves to Spirit or Inner Wisdom, we tune ourselves to that higher Wisdom Center as the guide for our life in that moment. Somehow this process happens between being and doing, arising when we choose where we place our attention and intent, and not "pushing" to make something happen. By consistently choosing this attunement, we come to know ourselves more deeply over time and to align ourselves with the deepest part of who we are.

When we are Mindfully Attuned, the task at hand moves from "doing" something or "getting through" it, to a meaningful process or relationship with someone, enhanced by our full attention and caring. I noticed this kind of experience in small or seemingly inconsequential activities. I tried to help my mother with everyday tasks as though she herself were holy. I did not think about it this way at the time, but as I reflect now, that is how I tried to be with her. It helped that I had deep respect for how she lived her life and that I loved her dearly. Helping her eat, moving her, or washing her face with a warm washcloth were not just tasks, but moments of deep service, a way to embrace life in a profoundly respectful manner that honored life and the opportunity to serve while on earth. Bringing this intent mindfully into activity brought forth the best in me at that moment.

The relative quiet of our living space allowed more presence in the moment, facilitating this attitude of treating life as holy. She had a single room, chose not to have TV access, and ate her meals in her room, feeling too embarrassed by her decreasing ability to feed herself. It was almost a sanctuary in which this kind of attunement more easily flourished.

During this time with my mother in her journey from this life, I increased my intention to be fully present in life. The challenge of the circumstances created a crucible for me that demanded intensity of focus and purpose. I find it challenging to maintain that kind of focus in everyday busy life. The concept of Mindful Attunement, in fact, came to me as I was watching myself play a computer game – over and over – in the middle of the night a number of months after my mother's death. I noted how different my experience of that moment felt than what was present during the last month's of my mother's life. When I asked myself how I could maintain the experience I found so meaningful before, I realized the importance of attunement to depth in the moment. With that realization, I turned off the computer and went to bed. That may not have been the deepest attunement, but it was certainly more consistent with my deeper Inner Wisdom, and more in alignment with my best way of living than mindlessly playing a computer game.

Developing Mindful Attunement requires commitment, making time for mindfulness as well as intentional attunement to Inner Wisdom or Spirit. I seek quiet times of the day, make time for a daily mindfulness practice, and sit with Spirit in prayer, so that a deeper level of attunement has a chance of moving into the day. Many things bid for attention, things that have much less depth and subtlety. Can I possibly stay deeply attuned in the way I felt in the crucible of my mother's dying? Not yet. I commit to bringing myself into contact with life as it is, accepting the moment, and reminding myself of what it can be. I also commit to reaching moment-by-moment for the expansiveness of the possible, where the giving and receiving seem to flow into something that is greater than the situation and the people involved. We must work with what is in front of us. I have seen what is possible and now seek to guide myself toward that deep connection with life and the Inner Wisdom which is always available.

THE BROADER PERSPECTIVE

Mindful Attunement brings us to the inner core of the labyrinth and the wisdom center of ourselves. The Inner Wisdom in that core can surprise you with its profound insight and guidance. It is the well from which you drink so that you take a kind of knowingness with you as you continue your journey, walking the labyrinth of life again and again, a different journey each time.

Mindful Attunement lights your way when you choose depth. This choice recalls you to the path of your highest purpose when you become aware of moving into less conscious and less mindful ways of being in life. Attune Mindfully by choosing to experience the deepest part of life – It is always beckoning.

QUESTIONS YOU MIGHT CONSIDER

❋ What is the deepest attunement you have experienced in your life? How would you put that into words?

❋ Describe the deepest level of attunement to which you aspire in the present moment.

❋ What would your life be like if you lived at that depth all of the time?

MINDFUL ATTUNEMENT EXERCISES

ATTUNING IN THE MOMENT: At the beginning of a day, choose a time you will check in with yourself. When that time arrives, take a moment to become quiet. In whatever way is right for you, attune to the deepest Inner Wisdom you can access and sit with it for a minute or so. Now, from that place, make a decision about what you will do, think, or say in the next moment that feels most in alignment with the quiet space you just found. Repeat this exercise as you feel is right.

MINDFULNESS PRACTICE: Decide how you want to incorporate a daily mindfulness practice into your life. Choose an actual time of day so that you can be consistent. You may choose to watch your breath or use tapes such as those by Jon Kabat-Zinn mentioned in the Introduction. Commit to a daily practice, and then return to that practice, again and again.

Chapter 16:
CONCLUDING COMMENTS

Mindful Resilience is a process. The components I have described are not experienced in a linear sequence. Instead, they dance together, forming a web of support for the journey. Mindful Presence, the underlying simple and profound experience so beautifully described by others, is the underpinning of everything else. The journey of Mindful Resilience is about fully being in the challenges, and moving through that process with grace. In writing I have attempted to clarify the aspects of this process that facilitated my own resilience.

I have extended the concept of resilience beyond just restoring some prior status, to growing in a significant way. This extension requires a Mindful Commitment-to-Transformation. That intent establishes momentum and direction along which movement can flow, with clarity provided by one's values. Mindful Equanimity is needed to support this process, for we cannot cope with repeated challenges unless we can create and maintain an inner calm, even in the midst of strong emotions. Equanimity is the calm that holds the space, so to speak, while other voices and actions form and creatively re-form in the process. Mindful Alignment gives us a road map based on our values that we can consult as we move down the road, checking our location and decisions in the process of finding our way. In the journey we may move through rain and fog, snow and hail, and sometimes we might even find rainbows. Decisions in complex situations often call for Mindful Discernment, using our value-based road map as our guide.

The process of being fully present, even in the face of life's challenges, involves not resisting but welcoming the world and its inhabitants, Mindfully Embracing what is, just as it is. That includes accepting our own imperfection and tendencies to stumble on this path, always new. In Mindful Embodiment, we fully step forward into the moment so we feel in a type of flow with life. We are able to see life's gifts or "miracles," and gratefulness weaves its way among the tears and struggles.

Our movement along the path we create is facilitated by awareness of our needs and those of others, continually refining the process of Mindful Awareness-to-Balance. We are never truly independent, and our connections to others offer the opportunity to build our capacity for Compassion. This web of relationships provides both support and more challenge, sometimes in the same human form. Mindful Compassion-to-Connection brings awareness of our innate connection, and a caring response to our relationships, bringing greater meaning to our lives.

Then the process of Mindful Attunement can connect us to Inner Wisdom or Spirit. This part of living, perhaps, is not seen with our limited physical vision, but rather in many different ways sensed through an innate knowing. It guides us, bringing power through Presence, intuitive guidance from its whisperings, and awe from its beauty. The inspiration arising from Mindful Attunement, mixed with the lessons from our challenges, both guides and supports growth into our most expanded self – or Self – in Mindful Refinement. Life invites us on that path of difficulty and deftness, challenges and creativity, tiredness and transformation.

May this book help you find your own path. Take what helps you and leave what doesn't engage you now for another person or another time. Only you can decide what is best for your life, now and as it unfolds. Your unique self requires its own journey and offers its own gifts to the world. May we all join lives to create a kinder and more generous world in which to live.

Writing this book is part of my journey. I wrote during the year since my mother's death, and reviewing the time leading up to that event helped me process the losses. Reflecting and writing also helped give shape and substance to my thoughts about how resiliency works, integrating the psychology of adjustment and growth with the practice of mindfulness and being present in life. I am grateful for what has come before, having found both renewed energy and a renewed sense of personal and professional direction in the lessons of life.

You are also part of this unfolding process. Thank you for your willingness to read this work and your openness to exploring the part of this work that is relevant to you. I invite your comments and thoughts about this book and the process of Mindful Resilience. You can contact me through my website: www.mndfulresilience.com where you can also find resources relevant to this work.

May you engage life's challenges with resilience, finding deep meaning in the opportunity of those moments, growing yourself and giving back to the world. May you find an inner calm amidst the storms of life as you journey toward the labyrinth's center.

NOTES

PART I: CONTEXT FOR THIS BOOK

INTRODUCTION: HOW THIS BOOK CAME TO BE

1. Mindfulness Meditation Practice Tapes: Series 1 with Jon Kabat-Zinn. www.mindfulnesstapes.com.

2. Kabat-Zinn, Jon (1990). *Full Catastrophe Living: Using the Wisdom of Your Body and Mind to Face Stress, Pain, and Illness.* New York: Delta.

CHAPTER 1: USING THIS BOOK FOR YOUR LIFE

1. labyrinth (2010) *In Merriam-Webster Online Dictionary.* Retrieved June 3, 2010 from http://www.merriam-webster.com/dictionary/labyrinth.

2. Reprinted with permission from the publisher. Text reproduced from *Labyrinths for the Spirit* by Jim Buchanan, copyright © Octopus Publishing Group Ltd, 2007, text copyright © Jim Buchanan, 2007, p. 9. All rights reserved. www.octopusbooks.co.uk/ and www.jimbuchananprojects.co.uk/. This lovely book introduces the concept of the labyrinth and gives excellent instructions on creating different kinds of labyrinths.

PART II: BASIC CONCEPTS

CHAPTER 2: RESILIENCE

1. resilience (2010) *In Merriam-Webster Online Dictionary.* Retrieved June 3, 2010 from http://www.merriam-webster.com/dictionary/labyrinth.

2. Jon Kabat-Zinn noted this movie quote in his book: *Full Catastrophe Living: Using the Wisdom of Your Body and Mind to Face Stress, Pain, and Illness* (1990), New York: Dell Publishing, p. 5. The 1964 film, "Zorba the Greek" (originally titled "Alexis Zorbas") was directed by Cypriot Michael Cacoyannis and is based on Nikos Kazantzakis's novel by the same name.

CHAPTER 3: MINDFULNESS

1. Reprinted with permission from the publisher. From *Wherever You Go There You Are*, copyright ©1994 by Jon Kabat-Zinn, Hyperion., New York. All rights reserved. www.hyperionbooks.com, p. 4.

CHAPTER 4: MINDFUL RESILIENCE

1. Siegel, Daniel J. (2007). *The Mindful Brain: Reflection and Attunement in the Cultivation of Well-Being.* NY: W.W. Norton & Company, p.6.

2. Siebert, Al (2005). *The Resiliency Advantage: Master Change, Thrive Under Pressure, and Bounce Back from Setbacks.* San Francisco: Berrett-Koehler Publishers, Inc., pp. 10-12. Note that these concepts are only some that Dr. Siebert identifies through his five levels of resiliency described in his book. His book is an excellent resource.

3. Reprinted with permission from the publisher. From *The Resiliency Advantage: Master Change, Thrive Under Pressure, and Bounce Back from Setbacks*, copyright © 2005 by Al Siebert, Berrett-Koehler Publishers, Inc., San Fransicso, CA. All rights reserved. www.bkconnection.com, p. 12.

PART III: MINDFUL RESILIENCE AS A LIFE WORK

CHAPTER 5: MINDFUL PRESENCE

1. The 1964 film, "Zorba the Greek" (originally titled "Alexis Zorbas") was directed by Cypriot Michael Cacoyannis and is based on Nikos Kazantzakis's novel by the same name.

CHAPTER 10: MINDFUL EQUANIMITY

1. Baer, Ruth A.; Smith, Gregory T.; Hopkins, Jaclyn; Krietemeyer, Jennifer; and Toney, Leslie (2006). Using Self-Report Assessment Methods to Explore Facets of Mindfulness. *Assessment*, 14 (2), 27-45.

2. The full first definition of equinimity from Mirriam-Webster Online Dictionary is "evenness of mind especially under stress." "equanimity." *In Merriam-Webster Online Dictionary*. Retrieved June 3, 2010 from http://www.merriam-webster.com/dictionary/equanimity.

CHAPTER 11: MINDFUL EMBODIMENT

1. Csikszentmihalyi, Mihaly (1990). *Flow: The Psychology of Optimal Experience.* NY: Harper & Row, Publishers, pp. 4-8. This book is a fascinating explanation of how one develops the internal state of flow. My understanding is that it is describing an internal state that impacts perception (e.g. passage of time). I believe that an internal state can impact our perspective on the world which can impact our own actions and thus the reactions from others. Whether Mindful Embodiment actually includes a change in the environment beyond this change in perspective is impossible for me to know.

2. Whether these experiences were felt as "miracles" because of my internal state or whether the external world had shifted, I do not know. I can only describe what I saw from my own perspective.

LaVergne, TN USA
19 November 2010
205624LV00010B/50/P

9 780984 598205